A LIFE INTERRUPTED

AUTHOR INFORMATION

Malachy Walsh is a retired civil engineer. After graduation from University College Cork he worked in England and Scotland. He later returned to Cork and eventually set up his own practice which grew to become a significant consultancy. Fully recovered, he now lives in Cork with his wife Pamela, where his hobbies include creative writing.

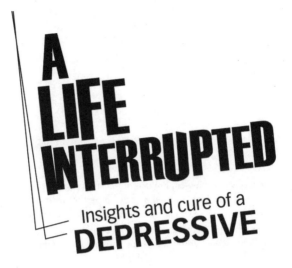

A LIFE INTERRUPTED

Insights and cure of a
DEPRESSIVE

Malachy Walsh

The Collins Press

Published in 2008 by
The Collins Press
West Link Park
Doughcloyne
Wilton
Cork

British Library Cataloguing in Publication Data

Walsh, Malachy
    A life interrupted : insights and cure of a depressive
    1. Walsh, Malachy - Mental health 2. Depressed persons -
    Ireland - Cork - Biography 3. Depression, Mental 4.
    Acupuncture
    I. Title
    616.8'527'0092

ISBN-13: 9781905172689

Typesetting: The Collins Press
Font: AGaramond, 11.5pt
Printed in Ireland by ColourBooks Ltd

The author wishes to acknowledge the support of Felicity Jones.

Dedication

To my wife, Pam, for her steadfast support throughout thirty years and more of living with a depressed husband: even on those occasions when I occasionally seemed to be much improved, she could detect the dread symptoms in my features. At every homecoming a cloud of gloom entered the house with me. The illness wrought havoc in both of our lives.

Enduring the silences, the downcast moods and my apparent preoccupation with self, she rendered vital support. Her energetic and cheerful presence in our busy household created the securest of refuges for me. She coped with me, fed me, ironed my shirts, managed the household and effectively reared our six children.

Twenty-five years later, following an entirely unexpected cure, further trials surfaced to test my wife. It appeared that my personality had altered yet again. In reality, it was my pre-depression self re-emerging. By then, that persona had been forgotten. To compound her problems, my old levels of assertion resurrected themselves, and these were in contrast to my depressed self who tended to acquiesce on issues.

In subsequent years, through her patient forbearance, I was able to write this book. Happily, writing it delivered a catharsis for me. Suddenly I was free to talk about my depression for the first time in two decades. This was yet another personality alteration, if a subtle one. Nevertheless she withstood the entirety of the successive challenges. Our marriage survived, thank God.

And to all who suffer in depression.

MW

Contents

Acknowledgements

Without his care, concern, and medications, I wouldn't have been able to keep going as a husband, father and employer. He was listener paramount. This fatherly man saw the struggling man hidden behind his depressed patient. Professor Norman Moore took charge of my hidden life and guided me past the menacing shoals that so often struck terror into my mind. His counsel steadied me when my life tended to lose its direction and despair threatened. I valued his warm concern and his remarkable ability to listen and hear every word. Years later, I was saddened to learn that he had died of Alzheimer's disease. The cruel irony of his fate was upsetting. His going left a void in my life.

How can I thank Ann Coleman enough for her courage in confronting me and forcefully recommending acupuncture as a cure for my depression? Amiable and good humoured, Gerry Longfield wielded the needles of an ancient Chinese medicine. His expertise and self-confidence delivered a cure. For his calm advice, and his cool guidance throughout my bewildering after-cure disturbances, I am deeply indebted. Using reflexology as a diagnostic tool, he treated my depression with acupuncture. He repeatedly encouraged his patient when my symptoms were resolutely resistant.

While I was advising on repairs to their monastery buildings, the nuns of the Carmelite Monastery in Tallow, Co. Waterford, became my long-term friends and intercessors. Their prayers for my health were answered.

Monsignor Michael Buckley DD, the healing priest, demonstrated the errors in my thinking and attitudes. Bluntly, he declared that my difficulties lay in my lack of faith. Shocked, I commenced searching widely for the meanings of both Faith and faith. I had lazily confused the two. Intensive and prolonged re-reading of his little book, *Why Are You Afraid?*, set me on a journey that culminated in an extraordinary six weeks of wondrous bliss.

Joe Dalton, a full-time lay intercessor, opened my mind to the wider possibilities of faith and prayer. He had sacrificed two successful careers in order to pray for others. His reassuring strength of personality, his positive counselling on prayer and the inspirational example of his way of life delivered a shaft of renewed determination to my wilting spirit.

How can I thank my closest colleague, Tony Moloney, who bore the brunt of my dark moods at work? Sadly, I appreciate the exasperation that I must have caused him. I haven't words to express my gratitude adequately.

For his patient reading of successive drafts of this book, I am indebted to my son Harry. His suggestions altered the book for the better.

Hugh O'Donovan, soldier, trekking leader, psychologist and friend, straightened my path in life when doubts caused me inner confusion. He gave generously of his time and encouraged me whenever events threatened reverses; I'm deeply grateful.

How can I ever thank God? Among the many graces I received, He sent these caring friends and others to render aid when my need was greatest.

Prologue

During my teenage years I began to ask myself questions. 'Who am I?' 'Do I really know this person who is myself?' 'What is the meaning of life?' 'Why do I exist?' 'What is existence?' 'What is being?' 'How is it that I can observe myself functioning at a task and at the same time listen to the sound of my own voice?' 'Who is this being that is me, who in all kinds of situations can at the same time observe this very same self in action?' 'Just who is this inner self, this "unchanging I" that I noticed?' These questions circled endlessly about in my mind.

Then I read somewhere of 'the unchanging I'. Seizing on to this concept, I pursued the identity of this silent spectator in vain. Eventually I just accepted this onlooker's presence as part of life. Scott Peck used the term 'the observing ego' in one of his books. It's so apt. It describes this human faculty perfectly.

Writing this book required many distressing return visits to past incidents in my depressed years. Marvellously, and over the long term, this laborious task delivered a catharsis. The emotional scars of the illness were healed in its writing. Today I'm free to discuss my illness with anyone, but the stigma attaching to depression creates in sufferers its own particular form of shyness, or reserve.

Depression affects one in ten. Its sufferers live silently and among the healthy, every day enduring but terrified to reveal the existence of their disease. While the stigma that persists prompts the unspoken query 'Is it madness?', the current level of media discussion on depression is a very positive development. It dilutes the stigma. Furthermore, I believe that the growing awareness of the relationship between depression and suicide promotes further understanding, in its own peculiar way.

Depression is an international problem. Visiting Australia some years ago, I was surprised to learn that it is endemic in that sunny continent. For many years, I was convinced of the beneficial effects of sunlight in this melancholy illness. However, this doesn't appear to be the case. In the countries of long nights, where depression thrives, it can be easily confused with SAD, or Seasonal Affective Disorder, a malaise that is widespread in Alaska, for instance. I experienced it as a mild but unrelated form of depression, and one that overlay my depression from late August until April.

The motivation to write about depression arose very soon following my recovery. It became a most compelling urge to help other depressives. Perhaps I felt guilty at the thought of so many sufferers not being healed. Prompted by a number of distressing and unsuccessful attempts at encouraging sufferers on a person-to-person basis, I switched to writing a book about my experiences. I felt that it might be a more appropriate way of offering help and encouragement to sufferers, their families and colleagues.

I must make it clear that I have no medical training; I practised as a professional engineer throughout my working life. This book is a layman's account of one person's experiences of depression. I don't explain the causes or the abstract working of the illness, for the simple reason that I can't. Others, including medically qualified sufferers, have written splendid books on this aspect of the subject. My own qualifications derive simply from a lengthy experience of the illness and its ultimate healing.

Part One

MY STORY

Depression — Its Onset

I t arrived by stealth. Unaware that my health was undergoing a profound change, I gave little thought to the possible implications of the succession of minor illnesses I suffered. Unnoticed, events crept up on me. I didn't connect one with the other.

Minor ailments afflicted me in my late twenties and into my thirties. Flu pinned me down regularly at Christmas. A stomach ulcer nagged for a number of years. I endured bouts of frustration, but their causes were unclear. For two years or so, I was gripped by an uncharacteristic lassitude, which was in conflict with my normal physical vigour. At work, relations between my late father's partner and myself were declining. Perhaps we had had enough of one another. I detected a shift in his attitudes. I didn't like what I intuited. Wholly dependent on my salary, I nevertheless sought an exit from the partnership. It wasn't going to be easy. I worried about the future. I hoped that these discomforts would pass. They didn't. They ultimately proved to be disguised harbingers of depression.

Then, in contrast, occasionally my mind and my cognitive processes would accelerate to a startling pitch. It suggested intellectual over-stimulation. While disconcerted, I wasn't overly concerned as I was able to slow it down. It might possibly have been a harbinger of a later manic state.

Erosion of my self-assurance and self-confidence created

difficulties. An inherent element of diffidence didn't help. In that era, psychology was not a commonplace topic of conversation. My parents might not have listened while I haltingly attempted to explain my innermost thoughts. My father was a remote figure.

I was born reflective. From an early age, I enjoyed mulling over the day's events: testing them, comparing them and seeking reasons for them. Usually I preferred to listen and observe rather than assert myself in discussions. At times, and paradoxically, especially with those I knew well, I would take charge and initiate a strategy and lead our youthful peer group on an adventure. Although I was nervous in some respects, when certain situations demanded it, I would assert myself almost to the point of recklessness.

When involved in play or recreation with my teenage friends, and when matters appeared to be getting out of hand, I would be the first to divert the group with reasoned argument. I was the conservative voice. Aware of these innate reactions, I sometimes pondered them. I didn't know whether it was fear of potentially disastrous consequences or common sense that dictated my caution. Overly impressed by my seniors and those in authority, I deferred far too readily to them.

My shyness frequently made life miserable. Anything remotely related to public speaking was far beyond my ability, and I remained in awe of those who were comfortable with it. Nevertheless, in later years, the sheer pressure of professional necessity nudged me on to the platform of public speaking. Gradually, and to my surprise, I managed to get over my inhibitions. Today I can look an audience in the eye respectfully and comfortably.

I never stood up to my parents. Stern disciplinarians, they left little room for constructive argument or reasoned debate. They were possibly replicating their parents' attitudes. The majority of the youth of my generation deferred to parents, and it certainly didn't occur to me to do otherwise, even though my younger brother, in his early twenties, began to assert himself and get away with it. I think he took my parents so much by surprise that they backed off. Maybe he unnerved them. In contrast, I was over-anxious to please my parents, and avoided conflict.

In the years before the arrival of our twin brothers, my younger brother was the favoured one of the family. He was a most attractive child physically and personally. Possibly his early years of affectionate parenting lent him a measure of useful self-confidence. Witnessing his later assertions, I despised myself for being so cowardly. I was far too biddable. On reflection, I just happened to grow up towards the latter end of an era of stern Victorian parenting.

From boyhood, I wanted to be successful, whatever that term may have meant. In my teen years, I won the annual school cycle race. A failure in all other athletic aspirations, I had built my own racing bike from a discarded one, having witnessed a cycle race. Instantly I recognised possibilities while the competitors circled the track. My training was intuitive. Over three or four months, and thrice weekly, I pedalled furiously on a five-mile out-and-home course. When the day came, I defeated the school giant in the last few yards. I was so fired up that nothing would have stopped me. I exerted such force on the pedals that I couldn't stand on dismounting. Dedicated to cycling thereafter, I competed in road racing and track events over a period of sixteen years.

However, while I was passionate about cycle racing, it proved to be a hard taskmaster. The competitive aspect of my nature drove me to compete. Even on training runs, I had to compete in being first over the crest of any hill along the way. I would punish my screaming muscles just to achieve that transient triumph. Lengthy hills, periods of high speed and fatigue often tested both my willpower and my physique. I learned to hang on at all costs, for the simple reason that my fellow contestants were also suffering. Furthermore, an innate stubbornness didn't permit me to give up. When some, particularly those I believed to be stronger than myself, fell back, I derived energy from the knowledge that I was stronger than they were on the day. Also, there were times when the shape of the race changed and I found myself, to my surprise, in an advantageous position as the finish approached. These occurrences illustrate how I was learning to cope with the bad patches in future life.

Nonetheless, while training for competitive cycling, I invariably over-trained. At the same time, I didn't ensure that I had adequate rest and sleep. The requisite self-discipline was missing. My anxious nature drove me to train at a near-racing pace instead of a steady, more comfortable pedalling rate. It was the regular accumulated mileage that generated form, but I didn't appreciate this. Furthermore, my training tended to be sporadic, and I wasn't allowing sufficient time for recovery between my efforts when I did train regularly.

My inherent level of ambition continued to play its part in my life. However, and despite myself, I steadily became a cautious tactician. I hesitated when I should have gone for it. Years were to elapse before I understood the source of this conservative attitude. Consequently opportunities were lost. The initial fire in my belly never regained its original intensity. Some unwanted inner force restrained me and I held back when I needn't have done. I no longer drove myself to exhausting all the strength in my legs. Did the prospect of the pain involved put me off? I don't think so. In time I learned to manage the pain of intense physical efforts, even to the point of looking forward to it.

Something also interfered with the essential discipline of training. I was easily distracted from such effortful undertakings by more diverting and indolent activities, and I often wasted my time in congenial and easy-going company. A compelling book proved irresistible, deflecting me from more appropriate efforts. I failed to discipline myself sufficiently to develop my physical talents properly through consistent training. The same lack of willpower invaded my studies.

As I grew up, the implications of success adjusted with my broadening awareness of life. Having a competitive nature was a positive help, even though I didn't appreciate this at the outset. Eventually my future career resolved itself into my becoming a successful consulting engineer. My dominant mood was cautious, apprehensive and worrisome. I believe that I was a moody person. As the earlier fire in my belly cooled, I would procrastinate instead of taking action. Naturally opportunities slipped from my grasp.

Even when events in my life were progressing successfully, a sense of unease taunted me. Periods of happiness or contentment were limited. Whenever I overcame challenging situations, I didn't celebrate. Instead I would cast about, anticipating the next challenge. To add to my discomfort, an innate pessimism intruded on my optimistic moments. My perpetual worrying and anxiety wasted both my nervous and physical energies. There were times when I worried about not worrying.

In my late twenties, I embarked on a solitary fishing expedition, wishing to experience the ocean in a small boat. Accustomed to fresh-water angling on lakes and rivers, I enjoyed handling boats. Now equipped with an unfamiliar line and bait, I anchored my hired dinghy at the mouth of Youghal Harbour. It was as much a personal adventure as a fishing expedition.

To my surprise, I hooked a big fish. It didn't struggle; it just exerted a steady downward pull on the line. I was deeply disconcerted, and my puzzlement somehow switched to worry and then to fear. No matter how hard I pulled on the line, the fish didn't stir. This was in total contrast to the fighting spirit of brown trout. In my imagination, the unseen fish grew in size. Time was passing, and I became worried. I was alone on the edge of an ocean. Suddenly, after endless waiting, the unseen fish stirred. Then, once I had brought it to the boat, it floated exhausted on its side.

At the very instant when I hauled this large salmon-like fish out of the ocean and into the boat, a distinct and new level of fearfulness invaded my being. I was afraid, caught in an uncontrollable and unattached fear. I had no idea of why or where it came from, but it became a permanent state. This sea-fishing incident was to become a determining harbinger of my illness. It was the initial manifestation of the onset of endogenous unipolar depression. Something from deep within my being had taken a chilling hold on my consciousness. It brought with it unwelcome levels of apprehensiveness, and was the commencement of a downward progression from a mild inherent nervousness to an irrational and unattached fear state that just wouldn't and didn't go away.

Some years later, following the successful completion of a large construction project for which I carried the design responsibilities, a series of complex physical and intellectual alterations overtook me. Two years of intense and pressured professional involvement left me tense beyond anything previously experienced. Normally such accumulated tensions passed off. On this occasion, they didn't. I simply couldn't relax. There was no sense of achievement or release at the successful completion of a major project. The realisation slowly dawned on me that something abnormal was happening.

Apart from the particular pressures and responsibilities of the project, I had been noticing a marked change in attitude in my partner towards me. He had interfered with the same project during my absence on holidays, something he had never done previously. This interference created difficulties with my client figures, causing me serious embarrassment on my return from holidays. I was deeply offended and perturbed. To my mind, it confirmed his unease at my increasing ability to see projects through to successful completions. The fact that my projects were of a different nature from those that my father and he had designed and supervised didn't help. He never explained this disruption, which was not in the least to our practice's advantage. The incident placed a layer of unease on my mind and undermined our relationship, which up to that time had been reasonable.

In or about the same time, I lost the ability to relax, even for a moment. I became hugely apprehensive and it seemed that I could neither think forwards or backwards. My mind was locked in a curious paralysis. It didn't affect all my cognitive processes, but current matters relating to work came to a halt. It was perplexing. At that point, I decided to seek medical help.

Reluctantly, on medical advice, I consulted a psychiatrist, who appeared oddly youthful to my mind. He listened and eventually told me that I was suffering from incurable unipolar endogenous depression. I was in my thirty-fifth year. It was a deeply disturbing diagnosis. When he mentioned the word 'incurable' my life changed in that instant. I had little idea of the fuller implications of his pronouncement. He prescribed medications, but offered little by way of explanation.

Unipolar is the medical term for the more common form of the illness. Bipolar is the term used for manic depression. Endogenous refers to an inner cause, rather than a depression brought about by external circumstances. In my case, I inherited a genetic predisposition to the illness. I was to learn very many years later, and long after my recovery, that both my father and his brother, my godfather, had suffered from depression.

A Quarter Century of Depression

I

Depression is an unrelenting, constraining, paining, lonely, morbid, distracting, separating, pessimistic, gloomy, sleepless and sombre illness. It is destructive of self-confidence. All of life becomes hugely effortful. Manic depression, in contrast, is a vastly energising yet relentlessly exhausting tirelessness. It is paradoxical in its unbounded energy levels, but its sufferers continue to desire rest. It renders sufferers incapable of relaxing or sleeping. Sounds great, but it isn't — far from it. It can cause its sufferers to lose their normal sense of prudence and responsibility, leading them to reckless undertakings, such as lavish overspending. On the other hand, it can render them hugely productive. I encountered three episodes of this manic state, as I will discuss later.

For me, facing the prospect of an utterly intimidating illness for the rest of my life was a mind-numbing shock. It was infinitely disturbing and vastly disappointing. My view of the future altered irredeemably in a matter of days. I just couldn't get my mind around the reality of being permanently ill.

The initial symptom was an all-pervading state of fearfulness. Unattached and relentlessly persistent, it rapidly metamorphosed to an intense pain in my midriff. Then I noticed a diminishment in my level of willpower. Life became more and more effortful. Inconsequential matters caused me frustration. The effort to shift my mind into action on a task — any task — and to do what needed to be done, assumed immense proportions. My mind seemed constrained by an invisible inner force, a mysterious restraint of the will. There was no shaking off this most unwelcome inertia. Each and every task became vastly effortful. Even the smallest and simplest ones necessitated a conscious decision of will to bend my mind towards doing the necessary.

This occurred at a vulnerable stage of my career. My wife and I were rearing six children, the youngest of whom was born within a month or two of the diagnosis. As unwanted events often dictate, the concurrence of two unrelated situations unfortunately made matters worse: I had just set up in business as a consulting engineer in my own right, thus compounding my pressures. Previously I had worked in a modest civil engineering consultancy with the man who had been my father's partner. However, as a result of the differences between us, I had literally walked out of a very successful practice in which I was junior partner. The practice had grown appreciably in the decade following the death of my father, and I had eventually concluded that my late father's partner and I were simply incompatible. Then, without warning, one day he asked for cessation of the partnership. I jumped at the opportunity and departed the office premises together with those people who had been working closely with me.

Now, stunned and confused by my recent diagnosis, I somehow coped with this new life, but not well. In time, on the insistent advice of a brother-in-law — 'You must go to Dublin and get the very best advice' — I consulted another and a more distinguished psychiatrist. This eminent Dublin-based figure recommended immediate hospitalisation. 'You're a very sick man,' he emphasised. 'It's the best course for you. You just cannot go on as you are.' Under his persuasion, I reluctantly and apprehensively agreed.

Instinctively I liked and trusted this new figure in my life. I wished to abide by his advice. However, it presented significant commercial risks. Potential clients might hesitate in awarding significant commissions to a depressive. Moreover, my wife and I had no surplus funds and depended entirely on my salary for our material welfare. The Voluntary Health Insurance — God bless it — saw us through the early years of my expensive treatments and hospitalisations.

II

In no time, it seemed, I awoke from an entire week's sleep, looking up at a high and unfamiliar ceiling in St Patrick's Psychiatric Hospital near Heuston Station in Dublin. I couldn't recall when or how I had got there. I had reached a state when work and its requisite demands were beyond my capability. Aware of the considerable stigma attaching to depression in the 1950s, I had nevertheless reasoned that the best course for me lay in hospitalisation. Working had become impossible.

Sharing a room with a charming and talkative manic depressive, I surmised that we were a good mix and possibly a deliberate pairing. He distracted and entertained me. Coming from a privileged background, he offered fascinating insights into a very different world from mine. He was a compelling conversationalist and, bit by bit, I pieced together his background and something of his illness. Not wishing to interrupt him, I lay back and listened. The fact that he was confined to the hospital premises, and his complaints at his mother's decisions to ensure this, suggested a dependence or related problems.

Altogether I spent eleven weeks in the care of the marvellous staff of that excellent institution and its related convalescent home. While hospitalised, I was being re-conditioned, as it were, to face the real world outside the boundary walls. That was the objective at least, but no one spoke to me about a new life handicapped by illness.

The hospital and its convalescent home became the securest of refuges from the harsh realities of a life coloured by pessimistic attitudes, and one in which I was harassed by the demons and pains of depression. Fortunately I felt absolutely secure in hospital, living daily among the staff and fellow patients. I loved the convalescent home in particular. Its setting among mature trees and broad green spaces suited my instinctive preferences for quietness and solitude. My inevitable and looming responsibilities were reassuringly far removed for the time being. 'I need time,' an inner voice repeatedly warned me.

My treatment comprised mealtime intakes of cocktails of pills and capsules. Some mild occupational therapy was also available. In hindsight, I believe that the unconsciously therapeutic socialising with fellow depressives was a significantly positive factor. I talked openly to fellow patients and compared notes on mutual symptoms. We had nothing to conceal from one another. I underwent ECT (electro-convulsive treatment) twice.

Under an anaesthetic, a bolt of electricity was discharged across my temples. When I awoke, there was no trace of depression. It had disappeared. Some may have witnessed a reconstruction of this treatment in the film *One Flew Over the Cuckoo's Nest*. For me it proved to be an adventure, almost a hilarious one in some respects. I was catapulted into marvellously sunlit spaces, high among sun-lit feathery clouds, and I lost all sense of responsibility – well, nearly all. I was absolutely relaxed and uncaring. I even boasted about my lack of caring to any patient who cared to listen. My poor wife was appalled and deeply troubled by this behaviour. She must have wondered whom it was that she had married. It was an utterly magical and spellbinding release, but sadly it was short-lived.

I entertained my fellow patients at mealtimes in the men's quarters, with a non-stop flow of quirky humorous comment, outrageous conjectures, theories and descriptions of imaginary events. I never stopped talking, contrary to my quiet nature, so much so that one patient suggested that I had been given talking pills. The dreaded realities of work and responsibilities lay far away, somewhere else, in distant places. Yet I felt entirely in control of myself in this new and companionable refuge.

Professor Moore, our psychiatrist, was Professor of Clinical Psychiatry at Trinity College and Medical Director of St Patrick's Psychiatric Hospital. A warm, sensitive and kindly man to his patients, it was he who insisted that I stepped entirely out of life on two occasions.

During each consultation, my depression was transcended for fifty minutes. Every patient was conscious of that fifty-minute allocation of his company; we would willingly have stayed for a hundred minutes. Invariably I was entirely absorbed in our dialogue. He listened as no other person had ever listened to me previously, and I was conscious of his focused attention. Each session ended with disconcerting swiftness, for the simple reason that this marvellous man was giving me his entire attention. His other patients experienced an identical temporary release. We were his idolising fans.

In the course of this first hospitalisation, I mentioned to Professor Moore that I sometimes consumed a little brandy before going to bed. I believed, in my profound innocence, that it would accelerate the onset of sleep. My psychiatrist was instantly alert at this and questioned me closely about this practice. He instructed me to attend the Alcoholics Anonymous sessions. Very quickly I concluded that this was a mistake on his part. I found these sessions to be extremely depressing. At that time, I actually drank very little, having first begun to drink alcohol only in my thirty-fifth year. Later I convinced Professor Moore that I had no attachment to alcohol, and he immediately released me from attending the classes.

Time passed swiftly. Then one day, during the fifth week of hospitalisation, my psychiatrist announced that I could go home. 'I'm very pleased with your progress,' he said. I was stunned and absolutely terrified at this abrupt and intimidating prospect. Part of me felt like running away, to anywhere. 'You'll cope, I know that you will,' he assured me, as I mentally struggled to face up to the prospect of work, and my many responsibilities in the bigger and challenging world outside. Deep down, I was hugely alarmed and uncertain that I would ever be able to cope.

Such was the progressively paralysing effect of the ever-increasing pain in my midriff that, following four or five weeks of living at home and working, while tenuously coping, I returned to the convalescent home deeply chastened, and stayed there for a further five weeks. The treatments of my previous stay were repeated, including the ECT. Once discharged, I didn't return to hospital for a further twenty years. I just coped as best I could.

In hospital, I had begun to learn how I might attain a precarious balance of living within the constraints of this complex illness. In the course of time, this enabled me to live and work in a reasonable manner. All of this was the very beginning of strange and unexpected adventures of my mind.

My life as a diagnosed depressive was unfamiliar and bewildering and I found myself adapting on a daily basis. Gradually it dawned on me that I was now living in a totally different world from that which I had previously known. This unexpected and sombre world delivered menacing prospects, whichever way I viewed the future. I failed to live a day at a time, which would have been reasonable. Instead, I regretfully visited yesterdays and viewed all the tomorrows that I could possibly imagine, each more threatening than the next.

Unquestionably, it was a strange and surreal world. In a comprehensive sense, I had been exiled by depression. I had departed from the familiar places and preferences of the past to darkened and bleak locations, while my inner world was dominated by fear and pain. That was how it was and I struggled, stumbled at times, laboured haltingly and coped as best I could. In time, I detested mention of the word 'cope'. I resented my pills and capsules and their persistent chemical aftertaste. Life was an uphill and unrelenting endeavour. My responsibilities and pressures were many, and the illness magnified beyond reason all that was implicit in my everyday duties of family and professional life. I desperately and unceasingly yearned to be well once again. Above all else I desired to be healthy and replete with all the energies of a normal being. Simply to be fit, energetic, confident and reasonably self-assured became my unwavering and unrelenting hope. I hoped; I didn't believe that I would be cured.

III

As the early years of my illness years passed by, I observed myself edging further and further away from those close to me. I was living in a different world from theirs, a darkened and sombre place, and I deeply envied those who had avoided the underworld of depression.

In time, I learned that intellectual engagement with others on work-related tasks triggered a release from my awareness of current levels of suffering. The same occurred in a cinema while enjoying an absorbing film. The downside of these releases was the return to real life. Wham! Reality closed down when I left either an absorbing meeting or the cinema.

My symptoms were many. Pain was the primary discomfort, the pain of depression. It was a level of pain such as I had never experienced previously. Both body and soul, it seemed, were equally in pain. It was some years before I recognised this. How did I know that my soul was in pain? I can't explain this in words. Awake in the night hours, I had ample time to assess my level of pain. Repeatedly reviewing my experiences of suffering, I eventually discovered that the pain of depression differed entirely from the more normal encounters with the pain of injuries, food poisoning, toothache, earache, muscle cramp, and so on. Confirmation of the existence of soul pain was presented to me with clarity in later years when I suffered the acute physical pain of a kidney stone.

Depression brought with it something different, a unique element. I puzzled over this for months and months; maybe it was for years. Then it suddenly dawned on me that not alone was my body in pain but my soul also was also in pain. This accounted for the extraordinary level of suffering that I was experiencing. It just didn't compare with anything I had experienced previously. Some time later, while watching a television documentary in which a journalist was interviewing my psychiatrist, I sat wholly absorbed. The presenter happened to be a depressive also.

'And, Professor, what about the pain associated with depression?' he enquired.

My psychiatrist was sitting in an armchair in his gracious living room. He paused, composing his thoughts. 'The core pain of melancholia is the worst suffering known to man,' he announced in measured tones. Instantly, I felt an urge to stand up and cheer, shout and clap. At the time, I had been coping with depression for possibly a decade or more. It had become abundantly clear to me by then that non-depressives failed to understand, or even appreciate in the least, the trials, aloneness, loneliness, terrors, tensions, tortures and angst endured by depressives.

Depression kills as other serious illnesses can do. The pain of depression can reach such intensities that the sufferer cannot endure another single moment of it. Suicide too often is the final resort. It becomes the sole prospect of release from what they perceive to be the worthlessness of their existences. I was elated by this pronouncement on the television programme. It gave me an immense lift. It was making public a profound insight to the level of sufferings of the depressed.

I should explain that 'melancholia' is an old-fashioned word for depression. To my mind, it is more expressive of the illness than 'depression'. It evokes some of the hidden sadness, aloneness and loneliness of the disease.

The pain of my depression varied in character and intensity throughout the years of the illness. Initially it was an intensely sharp internal chest pain, extending upward from my abdomen and into my chest. It was, as I visualised at the time, like an inward and upward thrust of a saw-toothed bayonet. Following my initial hospitalisation, it metamorphosed to an all-embracing pain of varying daily intensity. It was no longer an acute pain, located in a particular organ, or limb. It was all-pervading, a part of my physical self. In the latter years of the depression, it progressively worsened. Eventually it attached itself to my thighs, especially at evening time. I would spontaneously massage them in vain, seeking relief.

In the purely physical sense there was another symptom. Steadily and almost unnoticed, I lost weight in the early years of the illness, shedding nearly two of my normal eleven and a half stone. On recovery, my body regained those missing pounds precisely, and within a very short time. My weight has remained static ever since until in very recent times when I shed seven pounds for no apparent reason — the effects of age possibly. This earlier and protracted loss of weight suggests the enormity of the stress accompanying depression.

In the course of a particularly bad spell, towards the latter years of depression, I lost my appetite for food. This was entirely contrary to my natural appetite and enjoyment of food. I couldn't face meals. It quickly occurred to me that I could lose even more weight. Should I lose any more it would have become apparent that I was in the grip of a sinister illness. My clients would surely notice it. This induced a new terror in my life.

Laboriously I forced myself to eat. That was how it seemed to me. I had to force myself to masticate the food I didn't want. Meals became formidable challenges. I have no recall of how long this food rejection endured. Some years afterwards, my wife recalled that period, telling me how I used to stuff myself at a furious rate once any food was put before me! 'You just couldn't get enough of it,' she explained. Yet, at the time, I believed that I was reluctantly and laboriously forcing the food into my mouth.

Depression is living with the brakes on, restraining one's intellect. Would-be spontaneity of action is constrained. An ever-present awareness of the enormity of the efforts demanded in completing tasks impedes decisiveness. Everything, even the very simplest of tasks, becomes weighed down by the immensity of the effort involved in tackling it and seeing it through to its conclusion. Spontaneity is shackled and held back by an invisible and insurmountable force. In effect, the will is baulked. Depressives are always consciously striving to mobilise themselves into action or reaction, just as the healthy unconsciously do all of the time. It's like endeavouring to think with a mind that is floating in an imaginary glutinous and sticky fluid.

Perhaps the best, or maybe the worst, example of this mind–body state is the extraordinary efforts that were needed for me to vacate my bed in the morning. The mind of the sufferer is dulled and weighed down by the waking hours' review of the endless dread prospects of the day ahead, and the relentless realities of each and every individual effort necessary to undertake those tasks.

The once relatively simple act of rising in the morning became such that it demanded a vast mental effort to vacate the warm overnight comforts of the bed. Every single day commenced with this taxing struggle. 'Will I? Can I?' my mind muttered to itself, as I strove to energise my limbs and will my body out of the bed, onto the floor and into a standing position. Having attained that, remaining standing was still effortful. It never became easy in all of the more than twenty-five years of my depression. Once dressed and standing, I then consciously had to will myself to walk away from the bedroom. It was the final act preparatory to facing down the day ahead. It highlights the old phrase 'Sure, he took to the bed', so often used in previous years in protective references to the illness.

The still-warm bed continued to exude a powerful allure such that it absolutely had to be resisted, no matter what the effort. More than anything else, the depressive desires to retreat into bed, curl up in the foetal position and pull the bedclothes over his or her head. I didn't ever do that, though, knowing that if I were to do so, I would inevitably lose the overall struggle of meeting the multiple obligations in my daily life. Giving in to this temptation could mean losing out on living a useful life.

Depression assaults the will with an unceasing stream of negative mental suggestions: 'Another time will do'; 'Put it off

for a while'; 'Take a break'; 'This task or that is just too much
— pass it on to someone else'; 'Leave it until after the holidays';
'After the weekend will suffice — you just haven't got the
energy at present.' My sagging will was only too receptive to
such prompts. The consequent procrastinations were
sometimes destructive. Opportunities were lost.

Eventually, on recognising the inherent hazards of this
intrusive disorder in my life, I pulled myself together and
became alert to the subtlety of these temptations. With all the
effort that I could muster, I would bend my mind to the task
at hand and somehow battle my way through it. Whatever the
cost, the depressive has to carry on the struggle of living single-
handedly, as it were, while all the while appearing to be a
normal, active and healthy person.

It wasn't always a win–win situation in the early years, but
I adapted gradually, learning as I ceased yielding to these
negative temptations. In time, I achieved a dominant but
hugely effortful win–win pattern when confronted with
unfamiliar tasks, adapting by wilfully funnelling any available
energy into current tasks at the very start of the day. This
helped enormously. The momentum thus activated carried me
on well into the late afternoon. By evening time, though, my
accumulated tiredness induced a particularly downbeat
depression of mood. By the grace of God, I battled on.

IV

In the early years of the illness I learned the absolute necessity
of behaving normally. On one of the very rare occasions when
I confided to another the extent and painfulness of my illness,
I was rebuffed and criticised for failing in those things I had
once done well. This incident alerted me to the fact that those
close to me didn't wish to hear the details of my illness. Rather

it seemed to me that they simply wished me to be the person I had once been. As I performed, so I would be accepted. In effect, I became an actor. There was little alternative.

While life verged on the impossible, I was learning that the essence of my illness lay in mood swings, especially in the early years when my moods swung up and down for no apparent reason. My psychiatrist explained that chemical, or biochemical, changes in my brain brought about these swings, but such explanations did not help. I had always been a moody person who could be up or down, often for no apparent reason. Now my moods had taken control of my life. I couldn't manage them no matter how I tried.

Unexpectedly, despite my severely depressed state, I noticed that certain normally pleasurable experiences became intensified to an extent. Novels, music, films and even scenery were vivified. I gained new and enhanced levels of joyfulness — even at times tinged with excitement — from certain familiar recreations. It was as if my pleasure-sensing perceptions had been magnified. It was incongruous in the context of depression.

This unexpected source of pleasure reminded me of the advent of 'Technicolor' films. I recalled how colour heightened the enjoyment of films remarkably. In its time, it had brought a new dimension to enjoyment of the cinema. This vivification phenomenon affected me in a similar manner, and the unexpected experience of greatly enhanced enjoyment was most welcome. It lifted me temporarily whenever I participated in a favourite recreation. I experienced an inner measure of joy unlike anything previously experienced. It was marvellous while it lasted all through the lattermost years of the depression. I used to wonder if it might have been a compensatory offering from God, for the purpose of easing my sufferings. It certainly was a source of comforting reassurance, suggesting, as it did, the possibility of divine intervention.

Observing this new phenomenon closely, I noticed that books by certain authors, particular pieces of music, films and even scenic places delivered this new and greatly heightened enjoyment. While it was a marvellous surprise in its time, it continues to puzzle me, and to date I've failed to uncovered any explanation.

I first noticed it in Italy when I was climbing steep stone steps upwards from the quays of Portofino Harbour. There were large decorative plants to one side of the steps, characterised by furry and elongated leaves. It was summertime and the leaves were already dusted with the debris of the season's dry air. Somehow these plants, and the steps themselves, were abruptly vested with an unexpected beauty, so much so that they touched my soul and filled me with an inexplicable joy. I didn't know what to think or why indeed this sensation should strike me so forcefully. At another time, I possibly wouldn't have noticed either the plants or the steps. Yet I was hugely drawn to them and their appropriateness on one steep side of the harbour environs. Such was the impact of this discovery that I never forgot that otherwise incidental detail. Certainly Portofino itself was a factor. I was entranced by the place, clinging as it does to the face of precipitous rock slopes that plunge abruptly into the sea.

Then I experienced similar reactions while reading certain books, particularly novels, listening to certain pieces of music or watching absorbing films, particularly those whose theme music afforded a further attraction. It was absolutely marvellous, difficult to describe and frustratingly inexplicable. In a way, this new sensation injected vivid splashes of pleasure and colour into my very much white-grey-black world of depression. It added fleeting injections of passionate enjoyment to my otherwise drab and uncomfortable life.

Yosemite National Park in the US was a dramatic manifestation of this blessed enhancement. So also was Muir Park close to San Francisco, with its redwood trees. My enduring attachment to the National Park in Killarney benefited me similarly. Wintertime and snow-clad Zermatt, in Switzerland, was also positively affected by this wonderful phenomenon. Snow had always lifted my spirits to a extraordinary degree. It generated an inner excitement. During my depressed years, this enjoyment also was similarly enhanced. Forests increasingly reassured me by their shadowy stillness and their comforting massing of trees. Aware of the energy of nourishing fluids pulsating in their trunks, I somehow felt secure in their company.

Similarly, the film *Butch Cassidy and the Sundance Kid* touched me deeply for reasons I'm unable explain. Happening to revisit it on a DVD recently, I found it a disappointingly ordinary film in comparison to viewing it while depressed.

In the post-war era, I underwent a romantic attachment to Russia. This attachment was further augmented by my fascination with Tolstoy's novels. The novel *Dr Zhivago* haunted me for years. Possibly the despairing theme and the hopeless circumstances of the two central figures touched some sensitive nerve in my imagination, to an extent that I identified inordinately with them. I read the novel several times on first encounter, but the film brought it so much more vividly alive for me. I sat through it on at least three occasions, if not four. The music of its Lara theme still moves me today.

Andrea Giovene's books affected me likewise, but with extraordinary vividness. *The Book of Giuliano Sansevero, The Dilemma of Love* and *The Dice of War* all fastened themselves on my imagination by their vividness. Ernest Hemingway's novels entirely and compellingly absorbed me for a long time, too, until I began to see them in a different and perhaps more mature light, especially when free of melancholia. Their macho attractiveness and Hemingway's writing no longer impress me today, as they once did.

I loved *The Leopard* by De Lampedusa. Its Sicilian imagery still haunts particular corners of my mind. *Brideshead Revisited*, by Evelyn Waugh, affected me as few other novels ever did. I can't precisely explain why, but I relived its story intensely in repeated readings and in watching its excellent TV adaptation. Others of his novels delivered a similar, if somewhat lesser, magic. For a time, I couldn't read enough of Graham Greene's novels, especially the later ones like *Travels with My Aunt* and *The Tailor of Panama*. Anthony Powell was another novelist who infected me. I mention but a handful of those books and authors who came within the ambit of my empathising and heightened enjoyment.

Curiously and coincidentally, Hemingway, Waugh and Greene were depressives, too, to the best of my knowledge. Hemingway's suicide deeply disturbed me. His death severed part of my past. I was saddened at the level of suffering that this colourful and gifted character must have endured. I understood the compulsion to end his life by his own hand. I still wonder whether something in these men's writing communicated the existence of their illnesses to depressed readers like myself.

I commenced reading some of those books and viewing the films in the two decades prior to the diagnosis of my depression. What they wrote, or possibly even how they told their stories, appealed to a deeper part of my consciousness. Possibly some of the detail of my heightened enjoyment arising from depression was already merging with my recall of the enjoyments of earlier pre-depression years. My regret at losing this gift persists.

V

Medications eased the very worst of my symptoms. Without them, I couldn't have coped. This was dramatically highlighted whenever my psychiatrist changed my medication, a necessity I dreaded whenever it arose, as I had to cease taking the current medication for a week or more. Further, it took at least a further ten days for the new drug to take effect. This was horrific. In between, I was exposed to the unrestrained ravages of the illness. It was hellish.

Allied to the foregoing, I was forever feeling low, sometimes fatigued, and frequently gripped by a morbid anxiety. Sadness, loneliness, insecurity and apprehension about the future shuffled backwards and forwards. My levels of courage declined, as did both my self-confidence and assertion. Guilt of various sorts nagged at me. Despite these, I strove to displace my inherently negative outlook. There was also a persistent foreboding of an unknown and catastrophic event about to overwhelm me.

The insomnia characteristic of depression reduced my sleep to three hours at most. The remainder of nights was spent in the grip of the demons of depression, constantly evoking negative outcomes to the tasks confronting me on the following day. These were hugely exaggerated throughout the night hours. When the first signs of impending daylight filtered past the edges of the curtains, I was filled with terror. I simply didn't want the new day to arrive.

Winston Churchill once referred to his depression saying that 'the light went out on my life'. The aptness of this simile still impresses. The very word 'darkness' suggests itself whenever I attempt to explain depression. Grey skies were darker than they were in reality. Prospects were forever gloomy. The first signs of autumn and the irreversibility of summer's passing heralded a steep decline in my depression. I feared the arrival of autumn: a part of me died on its arrival.

My dislike of autumn endured from childhood. My parents had been enthusiastic in their appreciation of that, for me, most morose of seasons. They loved the turning colour of the leaves, and they certainly never voiced dislike. Silently, as I listened to them, I used to dread autumn's onset. Even at a young age, I had concluded that autumn was a season of the dying. Nature chose death as the days shortened. I hated to see the leaves falling.

In the years of severest depression, I could discern autumn's arrival as early as mid-August. I saw its imminence in the changing shadows of buildings on familiar city streets. I even noticed the weekly decline in the intensity of sunlight. My heart sank in sympathy.

Denial played tricks on my mind. Whenever the depression subsided and my mood swung upwards to a relatively comfortable level, I deluded myself into believing that I had recovered, and I would cease taking my medications. I felt so good that I was convinced I had been cured. This delusion was fuelled by the sheer intensity of my yearning to be well. I unwittingly slipped into denial, not once but repeatedly. Time and again, this irrational make-believe caused me needless suffering.

Inevitably the depression reasserted itself, plunging my mood downwards, together with its most unwelcome and frightening symptoms. The initial stages of each return of the depression were never readily discernible. It returned with its characteristic stealth. Mild irritability presaged its arrival. Most times I failed to notice this. Then I became convinced that some of those people working close to me had begun deliberately to harass me. Paranoia was taking over. I became irascible. Finally a sense of all-embracing frustration set in. Life became abnormally troublesome. As each of these changes manifested itself, I failed to recognise its implications until far too late. Then abruptly it would dawn on me what it was that was happening. My level of denial was such that it rejected all the incoming signals time and time again. The approach of the illness was unnoticed. Repeatedly it crept up on me and I failed to discern its imminent arrival.

I am unable to recall the precise moment of my acceptance of the reality of the illness. As far as I can judge, I persisted in repeated denials of the illness for as long as three or four years.

During the ten years or so following my diagnosis, the depression gradually worsened. Then it steadied for a period, to be followed by an inexorable decline. I knew that I was up against an immense challenge in managing to live a normal life. Living with the brakes on was akin to the effort of labouring up a long incline on a bicycle. This was the feeling that I identified with the all-pervading constraint on my mental functions, mostly on my willingness to initiate action.

It was so frustrating. The cognitive processes seemed to take far longer than in times of good health, requiring immense conscious effort. However, I believe that my intellectual resources performed normally. Judgments remained as before. Decisions took longer, and I had to make many serious decisions during the years of my illness, but the majority of these proved correct. I record this humbly. I did make mistakes, of course but somehow, and fortuitously, I avoided disastrous errors.

VI

Depression persisted throughout most of my professional career. The experience, even in retrospect, was appalling. I am incapable of conveying adequately an impression of the periods of sheer desperation and fear that I endured in situations related to work.

The working life of a consulting engineer is pressured, stressful and endlessly demanding. It is deadline-driven for the most part, with clients dictating the project timescales. At the outset, they anxiously await the imagined concepts set out and described in drawings, so that they can both study and test them. When a project moves on to actual construction, the emphasis shifts relentlessly to the completion date. It's understandable. There will be no return in investment until the facility is completed and in use. The prospect of delay becomes the unthinkable hazard.

Personal work-related confrontations were extremely difficult. Imposing discipline raised its own difficulties, especially when forceful assertion was necessary. My measure of assertion eroded as the depression deepened.

The one symptom of my illness that didn't escape the notice of acutely observant friends was my inner tension. I probably exuded tenseness. I realised eventually that even while sitting on a chair, I was poised for take off, my legs bent back under the chair preparatory to a quick exit. This was but one of the physical symptoms of the tension generated by melancholia. It was also demonstrated by my somewhat abrupt manner and, of course, in my strained features.

I walked rapidly or, rather, I hurried. I was edgy, and in the winter months there was greyness about my pallor. One or two commented on it, usually mentioning it sympathetically to my wife. One work-related acquaintance teased me about my apparent aloofness.

Nevertheless, in the everyday performance of my duties, I remained effective once I moved beyond the second of my initial two stays at St Patrick's Hospital. The mood swings were gently undulant at the outset. Sometimes then it felt as if the depression had lifted. At least, the symptoms weren't so intrusive that I couldn't transcend them. I recall good times while this state held, both in and out of the workplace. Learning to accept the reality of depression took as long as seven to ten years.

The scope of my practice's commissions ranged over a variety of civil engineering projects, bridges, marine structures, water and sewage schemes and a multiplicity of buildings factories and industrial complexes, including airport facilities. The variety of the work content was never less than stimulating. I found the design content of my work particularly fulfilling. Creative tasks attracted. Sadly it is in the nature of things that success as a consulting engineer means that inevitably one is nudged away from pure design and into the realms of management and administration. I was less than content in this latter environment.

The different projects that came my way, combined with their ever-changing geographical locations, injected a useful diversity to my days. I enjoyed the friendships that I made during the course of numerous projects. The constant change of location left little room for boredom. In and among all of this, there was an underlying buzz of achievement in the realisation of physical construction, from the concepts initially developed on CAD screens. The inevitable urgency of projects also injected a measure of energising pressure, mixed up with anticipatory excitement.

The constant hunt for new projects created its own challenges. It was a succession in the winning and losing of metaphorical races, the prizes being valuable contracts. Winning a commission was a high point in the continuum of my working years. Current problems melted away in its inevitable surge of exultation.

Sadly, and all unexpectedly, the day arrived when, having

just won a new and valuable design project, the once-familiar elation at its confirmation failed to ignite. An inner voice insisted 'But you've done all this before. It's nothing new. You've been through it all many times. It's just more of the same.' This had nothing to do with my depression. It came from a different and deeper source within my consciousness.

On reflection, it was inevitable. Repetition numbs the emotions. The race to establish myself and the practice had by then been won. I accepted that I had arrived, as far as my professional career was concerned. The practice that I had founded had become well known. Now there was nowhere else to turn for comparable stimulants and excitements, other than continuing to survive commercially. It was an unanticipated disappointment.

Possibly the depression hastened the arrival of this unwelcome ennui. It may have been connected to the 'greyness of the soul' that is sometimes mentioned in religious biographies. However, in this instance it related to the non-spiritual material world.

In the course of my work, I made a regular out-and-return journey. I knew the roads well. At one point, my route crossed a range of low mountains. Being an enthusiastic driver, I pressed on enthusiastically, especially when alone. I was described as a 'fast but safe driver' by passengers who had experienced my urgent driving. One was a Formula One driver who instructed me during a high-speed driving course on a racetrack, and refused to believe that I had never raced previously.

I recall one occasion, when I was making this journey, and, on cresting the familiar mountain range, I set the car up to negotiate a familiar bend. I had negotiated it many times, but suddenly the rear wheels slid sideways. Correcting swiftly, the car then slewed to the left. Correcting again, the car slewed to the right. Working frantically at the steering wheel, I managed to keep the car on the road, but I couldn't slow its progress. A lorry appeared dead ahead, labouring uphill under a heavy load. My car hit its robust bumper head on. I saw the startled expressions of the driver and passenger as the black-painted bumper raced toward the bonnet of my car.

In the brief moments of unconsciousness, I experienced a blissful and vast sense of release. I believed that I was dead. All was brightness. The entirety of my worldly cares, troubles, worries and sufferings was gone, securely left behind in the mortal world. Momentarily I experienced a limitless happiness. Then, as the very first glimmerings of returning consciousness took hold, I absolutely did not want to return to this planet Earth. Fleeting moments of the deepest of disappointment ensued.

I came to, to find the rear wheels of my car on the left-hand ditch. The lorry was unmarked. Fortunately, although it was long before seat belts became mandatory, I was wearing one, out of personal conviction.

That momentary experience of the world beyond death remains stamped indelibly on my mind. The marvellous sense of escape to the ultimate refuge, from the trials of this life, endures in my mind.

Towards the end of my illness, perhaps twenty years or so following on the diagnosis, I received an extremely urgent and challenging commission. This client demanded that the construction of a multi-storey car park commence on site within an incredibly short period of time. In normal circumstances, three months might have been a reasonable period for the preparation of the necessary designs, drawings and documentation. However, this client insisted that the contract documents — drawings, specifications and bills of quantities — should be completed within two weeks. It was an abnormal challenge. However, at the time, work was in short supply, and this commission could not be turned down. We needed the fees, and I had to accept it on the terms offered.

I divided the staff into two groups. We were to work from 7 a.m. to 10 p.m. One half of the engineers and draughtsmen were to work exclusively on this car-park project. The remaining half of the office design staff had to keep all other projects going. At the same time, they were not to intrude in any way or distract those who had been allocated to the car park.

Meanwhile, I immediately commenced preparing an itemised task list for each design engineer involved. On completion, I used it as the checklist for the items comprising the bill of quantities, which document I began drafting. While we had no more than two weeks for the completion of the task, I informed the staff involved that we were going to complete it within twelve days, as there inevitably would be last-minute adjustments to be made.

The drawings, bill of quantities and specification were delivered on time and on the hour, much to the surprise of the client's engineering staff. This project occurred within eighteen months of my re-entering hospital, having managed to stay productively on my feet for almost twenty years following my first hospitalisation.

This assignment is an illustration of how the mind of a depressive can remain usefully productive. History provides countless examples of this. On a far larger scale, Abraham Lincoln, a President of the United States, was a depressive, and he coped with a civil war. Churchill, as mentioned above, was another, referring to his depression as his 'black dog'.

I rarely missed work because of the depression. Passing illnesses like flu might keep me in bed for a day or two, but it was only in the latter years of the depression, when my psychiatrist insisted that I re-enter hospital, that I missed work. Altogether I was missing from work for two fortnightly intervals. The getting-up-in-the-morning daily crisis never prevented me from arriving at my desk on time. I actually lost very little time during the quarter century duration of the illness.

My diminishing powers of concentration, however, became a handicap when the depression spiralled downwards towards its worst phase. I countered this by having vital documents checked by others. As far as I can judge, the loss of normal concentration emanated solely from the depression. So many negative thoughts and possibilities plucked at my attention; these, combining with my perpetual state of unease and angst, made it necessary to indulge in continuous self-assessment of the level of my attention to each task in hand. My mind rarely rested in repose, except when absorbed in a writing task. A continuing sense of foreboding about some future and unknown catastrophe didn't help. I knew that this was irrational, but it was so damned insistent, an unwanted distraction.

An irritating and demanding impatience countered my desire to work methodically. I was hugely impatient to reach the end of tasks. Apart from this, a pervading restlessness presented itself in the form of a perpetual anxiety to be somewhere else or at least to be on the move to another location. If I remained some time in one place, I became edgy and needed to be on the move once more. This pervasive restlessness took its toll on my energy resources. Fortunately it diminished with the passage of time.

I couldn't commit myself to intellectual or physical tasks unless, with a deliberate and conscious effort I first mobilised my constrained will to act. Spontaneity of action was damped down. Practically all of life was effortful because of this. When confronted with an immediate task, I had to bend my innermost self forcefully to get on with it. Sometimes I would mentally walk around and around it, nerving myself up to tackling it.

The stimulus of people around me and involved with me was unfailingly helpful. The group's dynamic both motivated me and led me almost effortlessly at times into action. Work-related verbal interaction also kept my mind both occupied and energised. This is not to say that people didn't get on my nerves. Some certainly did, and the depression definitely made me irritable and at times irascible. It also played up my tendency to be a serious-minded person. My judgmental tendencies didn't help either.

VII

For the depressive, personal conflicts are exaggerated in their prior implications. It seemed to me as if the depression induced anxiety states that intensified prospective inter-personal confrontations. I had to steel myself to confront whomsoever might be involved. Oddly, doing so was easier when the difference of opinion involved an injustice. I'm not sure why this should be so, but instances of injustice angered me, thereby apparently energising my will.

Touching on the word anger, depression certainly damped down my ability to become angry. In time, I accepted this as symptomatic of the illness. I couldn't do anything about it. I was fully aware of this inability but that didn't help. A measure of controlled anger can be useful on occasions.

I recall a day when I was so bothered, harassed and stressed that I rested my head in my hands and asked myself if I was going mad. I dreaded the prospect of losing my mind, but it seemed on that occasion that I was beset with such an abnormal accumulation of demands on my energies and willpower that I was losing my self-control. Fortunately that nightmarish reflection passed on.

There were other bad times as well, when I was terrified at the notion of losing control of my mind. The spectre of a nervous breakdown haunted me for years. The chilling thought of being confined in a mental home would surface from time to time. Thank God, events never came to that.

In this disconcerting climate and in praying for a healing, my wife and I had commenced attending daily Mass. Our prime concerns were my health and our family's welfare. We had to provide for the growing needs of their emerging lives. Education, recreation, clothing and holidays were just some of the things that had to be paid for. The children hadn't reached their most expensive stages at the time, but we knew that the demands on money would increase.

Then one day it occurred to me that an element of self-help was imperative. The expression, 'God helps those who help themselves', echoed in my mind. Observing my declining energy levels under the influence of the depression, I recalled my years of competitive cycling. During that era I had enjoyed vast energies. Intuiting that a high level of fitness would be beneficial, I told myself that it might even go so far as to improve my health.

Experience indicated that cycling would be overly time-consuming, so I tried skipping for three or four months. It was boring, though, offering little distraction. While persisting at this experiment, I pounded a deep depression in an area of tarmac in the garden. Finally I decided that the most efficient form of exercise had to be running. This challenged me, as responsible people approaching early middle age did not run on public roads in the early 1960s. No one did. Commencing in an autumn's declining days, I ran on neighbourhood footpaths and roads under the cover of darkness. Then, as the days lengthened with approaching spring, I closed my mind to my neighbours' startled looks and kept on running. My misfortunate wife endured these embarrassments silently. My daughters screamed whenever I mentioned that I had met someone whom they knew while I was jogging.

It wasn't easy. Three months of straining lungs and aching muscles were endured before I was able run a mile in reasonable comfort. Gradually I extended my circuits until I ran for forty minutes, free of undue physical distress. A warming sense of satisfaction and a sense of release grew as my fitness increased. Climbing stairs became effortless. By the end of a year of running, my energy levels had improved perceptibly.

Today I sometimes wonder at the possibility that retirement from competitive cycling might have accelerated the onset of depression. It followed remarkably close to my retirement from the bike. Cycling had been a most fulfilling activity for me. Its combination of travel and exercise were appealing and it also gave expression to my competitive nature. Its absence created an unwelcome void. I had innocently anticipated being able to channel the consequent surplus energies into my work, but the reality was the opposite. In the absence of exercising, my energies dwindled bit by bit. I had actually overlooked this as a possible result.

I ran prior my evening meal. Showered, changed and seated at the table, I was pleasantly relaxed. What was more, I slept longer after exercising. An element of confidence surged in my being. With the passage of months, my running improved steadily. Once out and warmed up, I experienced a sense of liberation. Not alone could I run, but I was free to do so whenever I wished. This may have been a temporary release from the inertia of depression. However, the effort of changing my clothes and dragging myself out to run continued to demand a strenuous effort of will. Once running comfortably, I all but forgot the symptoms of depression. At the same time, work-related challenges lost their menace. No matter what was occurring in my working life, I somehow transcended such difficulties and ran joyfully. Such positive, if temporary, lifts provided a most welcome source of encouragement.

In time, I learned that the tiredness in the aftermath of a day's work dispersed within the first mile or so of running. It was as if this tiredness was a temporary state. Later again, I noticed that genuinely challenging and deeply worrying work-related challenges often assumed more realistic proportions while I was running. On occasions, these would be accompanied by a sequence of positive solutions surfacing effortlessly in my mind. At other times, seemingly intractable issues unravelled themselves. This was magic, or so it felt. Other times, I experienced surges of self-confidence. All of these helped to prop up my wilting self-belief and determination. Aerobic exercising increased blood flow through my veins and lungs, thereby picking up energising oxygen along the way, or so I theorised.

It was a winter evening. I was running beside the River Lee and the lights of street lamps on the further bank were reflected on the river's dark waters. Abruptly I was conscious of the effortlessness of my running. My body was running while I relaxed and observed all that was around me. I could turn my head to left or right without upsetting the rhythm of my legs and breathing. There was no conscious effortful straining forward in order to maintain my pace. My body and limbs were running as if detached. I had become an automaton. It was an apart-from-body sensation.

By then, the running boom was manifest in in the US. I had been subscribing to a quality American running magazine whose medical correspondent was a doctor, a convinced jogger and a philosopher. He quoted Emerson frequently in his articles. He had begun to write about the physical and psychological benefits of sustained and arduous exercising. The expression 'runners' high' was coined during that same era. It was a consequence of the release of naturally occurring painkiller endorphins into the brain. Sustained and arduous exercising was the magic-maker, and this, coincidentally, was precisely what I was doing. The benign after-effects usually lasted until I fell asleep in bed.

In contrast to these happy discoveries, where in the past I had enjoyed attending engineering conferences and other gatherings of my professional peers, suddenly such occasions posed menacing challenges. For no obvious reason, I was reluctant to confront my peers in numbers. My innate self-confidence, such as it was, had evaporated. Instead, in the company of my peers, I felt hugely inadequate and insecure. While everyone around me appeared composed, controlled and confident in themselves, I was, in contrast, uncomfortably uneasy. I had to force myself to attend such events. All the pleasure and ease in the company of my fellow engineers evaporated. It was as if I were among a gathering of vastly superior strangers.

At some time in those darkest years of struggling to cope, an incident occurred that remains clear in my recall. All through those years of struggle, I prayed for a cure. My religious beliefs never wilted. My meagre measure of faith did. I turned to God for help. My praying became more organised and with it my reading of inspirational and religious books. I was determined to find a cure.

My wife was going on a holiday with close friends and very much with my blessing. I fully appreciated that she needed a break from living day to day with me. I encouraged her in this, and this worked well until the time when this particular annual holiday neared. By then it had become an established routine, a phase in our mutual year. One day, a week or so prior to her departure, I was filled with terror at the prospect of her absence. There was no other word for my fearfulness.

At that time, the depression had dipped to a darker phase. I absolutely did not want her to leave me on my own at home. I believed that I wouldn't be able to cope but I didn't mention my feelings to her. The days passed while I observed myself grappling with this new and fearful apprehension. A large part of me didn't want her to go while the other part knew that she had to go. This internal tug-of-war persisted until I had delivered her to the airport and to her friends. She departed on a Saturday. It was in late May or early June.

Early on that Sunday morning, I was preparing my breakfast, deeply conscious of my aloneness and vulnerability. Organising myself, and observing self at the same time, I prepared my breakfast, wondering at my ability to cope. On the dining table my organiser lay open at the page headed by my most inspirational and favoured quotation. Walking toward the table, that familiar quotation was illumined by an intense and shimmering light. It was such that it far exceeded the brilliance of that June morning's sunlight bathing the entire living room. It was a combination of direct sunlight and its reflected rays from the surface of the sea. Yet the intensity of light on the page was of a brilliance far exceeding it.

In an instant I knew that it had to be the much-repeated words: 'If thou canst believe, all things are possible to him that believeth.' I wasn't in the least frightened, not even disturbed. On my arrival at the table, the illumination disappeared, but a glance at the open page confirmed the inspirational quotation.

A gentle surge of joy suffused my being. I knew then that I would be able to cope in my wife's absence. The frightening sense of terror declined. Things were not going to get any worse. They didn't and Pam returned, mentally and physically better equipped for the fray. I accepted this inexplicable occurrence as an instance of divine intervention. It conveyed a reassuring measure of hope for the future.

That terror, or a measure of it, sometimes recurs reflecting the intensity of the loneliness that can afflict the depressed. Aloneness is a more appropriate word, I think. Neither expresses fully the extent of solitariness that I experienced. Depressed, I remained alone in a silent and unspoken world. This state was typical of the symptoms accompanying my depression.

VIII

I wasn't a studious type. I disliked school, and found homework a stumbling block. I couldn't bend my mind to complete it. Oddly there was no parental encouragement, which is strange, given that my father was an academic. I drew fire upon myself. Sarcastic teachers teased me about my father's professorship. However, I enjoyed aspects of English, particularly compositions, and I looked forward to the challenge of an essay throughout secondary school.

Unfortunately the senior English teacher didn't believe that I wrote any of my submissions. This was frustrating. Did it impede the development of a very useful skill? The same teacher, in my final years in school, abruptly accepted that I had written my compositions, and later he took to reading them to the class. Had I met an encouraging teacher at an earlier time, I might well have become a writer — well, maybe. In later years, I became a motoring correspondent, which enabled me to test new models and write about them. Happily this fulfilled a yearning for both writing and driving the latest models of cars.

In a recent conversation with an acquaintance who is a long-term depressive, he told me that one of his most comforting recreations was writing. 'What do you write,' I asked.

'Oh anything; whatever comes into my head,' he answered.

'It brings relief from the depression. The content doesn't matter. It's just the writing that brings relief.' This statement intrigued me. I pounced on it, quizzing him at some length.

Writing helped me to transcend my illness. Over a period in the early years of my depression, I wrote five novels, motivated by the hope of finding an easier and an independent way of making a living. At that time, my depression was increasingly hampering my ability to work, and I wasn't certain that I could keep up the effort. In my naivety, I believed that writing novels would be much easier than managing a design office. I wrote five novels in longhand.

Early on Saturday mornings, I pursued this activity, uninterrupted for four hours in the quietness of the empty office. It was an intensely sustained effort. In my blissful ignorance, the objective seemed enormously desirable. Later on, while writing many drafts of this book, I noticed that when I got up from my desk following the writing, I was charged with considerable energy. I could hardly wait to expend it on my garden. I was, at the time, converting a steep ocean-facing slope into some semblance of a garden.

Why four hours of intense creative activity should generate energy is something that fascinates me. Tiredness seemed the more probable outcome. Possibly my level of absorption was such that the chattering of the discursive mind was stilled. Being freed of the endless stream of unsought thoughts, imaginings and worries that so disturb the wandering, daydreaming mind somehow stored up the energy otherwise misspent. This imaginary living — daydreaming in reality — occupying both the past and the future, regretting the outcome of unsatisfactory past events, reliving long-finished conflicts, or anxiously planning the exchanges in some future conflict, all combine to disturb and tire the person harbouring such uncontrolled thoughts. This so commonplace mental turmoil has to consume energy. The fact that the restless turmoil was temporarily stilled created a bank of energy.

In the same way, work-related writing tasks delivered a measure of relief from depression. It was a therapeutic activity, and had a calming effect on me. The depression never interfered with my ability to write, with the exception of a period when the illness was at its severest.

Through a fortuitous chain of circumstances, I became a motoring correspondent, and, for fifteen years, I wrote a motoring column for an engineering journal. During that time, I met an American journalist while on engineering business in Saudi Arabia. He turned out to be Peter, the younger brother of Paul Theroux, and we became friendly. Peter was a journalist at the time, and introduced me to an editor of the *Saudi Gazette*, an English-language newspaper published in Jeddah. The latter commissioned me to write a weekly motoring column. The pay was handsome and I pursued this for a number of years. Sadly, the subsequent decline in the Saudi Arabian economy, and the consequent reduction in the number of non-nationals living in the country, forced the newspaper to cut the number of pages in its issues. The expatriate population was dispersing. I received a nice note of regret from the editor, thanking me for my good work.

At the same time, I was also contributing to two motoring magazines. Cars and driving continue to be a passion with me. I still enjoy driving, and am deeply appreciative of the gift of individual transport. As a child, I was besotted with cars. My father's choice of cars was thoughtful. He was interested in motor racing, rousing his sons at six in the morning to watch the practice sessions of the inter-war Grand Prix racing cars on the Carrigrohane Circuit in Cork.

Writing can be a mental journey for me; bringing relief from everyday pressures. I found it a fulfilling form of self-expression. Each of the five novels I wrote was a journey of discovery in the unknown and untracked regions of my imagination. I didn't plan those novels. Rather, I wrote my way into each. At the outset, I had no idea of how they would end. Regrettably none were published, although publishers' readers were invariably encouraging. However, all suggested a rewrite, which was something I could not face. In my depressed state, I couldn't surmount the inertia that baulked me.

IX

In the 1970s, the Irish economy plunged into prolonged recession. Commercial survival became the main preoccupation of those in business. Money ran short. Cash flows all but dried up. In my practice, getting paid for work done became an unrelenting tug-of-war. A new and intimidating layer of stress attached itself to my working days. In this harassing climate, I learned more about my reactions to stress. Very simply, the greater the stress, the deeper my depression sank. As the economy of the country declined, so my depression dipped to new and terrifying levels.

In pursuing new commissions for the practice, I encountered formidable obstacles. Challenging in the past, marketing became vastly intimidating in its pressures and absolute-seeming demands. There could be no postponing the search for even the slightest hint of a new prospect, and there weren't many. Knowing that our competitors were in the same boat simply magnified the pressure.

My depression developed more sinister characteristics in reaction to this work climate. It spiralled downwards. The unwelcome arrival of paranoia really stretched me to my limits in coping. Its form of attack was insidious. Part of me would be convinced that one person or another was deliberately persecuting me at work. While I knew that such perceptions were more than likely untrue and no more than a paranoid delusion, yet each incursion was frighteningly convincing. It became a tug-of-war between my rational mind and the erroneous delusions that streamed across my consciousness. I checked out these delusions with my wife. Unfailingly she discerned the truth of those torturous suggestions. The paranoia persecuted me during the worst of the lattermost years of depression.

With renewed earnestness, I enquired of my psychiatrist if a cure were possible for my depression. He invariably fell back on his familiar response: 'I hope that I'll live to see the day when a white-coated biochemist discovers a pill that will cure depression. No, Malachy, there's no sign of such a prospect at present.' Occasionally he would remind me that no matter how hard I tried, there was no way that I could overcome the symptoms of my depression by an effort of will, no matter how I strained.

In the back of my mind, I had been wondering about the possibilities of person-to-person therapy, or cognitive therapy. I knew little about this other than what I read in the media. As far as I can recall, I never mentioned it to Professor Moore. I had an inner suspicion that a therapist might be able to unravel and clarify my thinking and strengthen my innermost convictions. This, I intuited, might enable me to rise above my current levels of harassment.

Abruptly the depression began affecting my eyesight. My immediate surroundings assumed different appearances. It was as if my physical world were moving closer to me, or the lenses of my eyes were re-focusing, drawing walls, buildings and the built world closer to my face. Everything within my field of vision, paradoxically, was at the same time shrinking dimensionally. This was extremely disconcerting. I would blink, look around and shake my head, but the effects persisted. They came and went in no particular pattern.

At a subsequent stage, an extreme physical tension gripped me, progressively becoming more acute. While the depression normally induced its particular tensions, this eyesight mal-functioning was different. At times, it was such that it seemed it must be visible to all. It was as if a finely woven screen had been placed in front of me and close to my eyes. I saw life through its mesh. So persuasive were these impressions that I believed those sitting close to me must surely have noticed this phenomenon. There were meetings when these manifestations made me squirm.

In coping with these distractions, part of my mind attempted to concentrate on the current issues. Mentally I balanced apprehensively on a knife-edge, fearful that someone was going to ask, 'What on earth is happening to you?' They never did. My worst apprehension was that of a total nervous breakdown during a meeting. Fortunately this never happened.

At some time during these struggles, I was to travel to California as part of a delegation charged with promoting new business investments for my home city. I had been feeling remarkably well at the time and it wasn't an onerous undertaking. It was simply a matter of contributing by one's presence. In effect, it was a holiday. Such breaks were precious respites. Unfortunately an unexpected and deeply stressful crisis intruded. Somehow I weathered it, or so I thought. Driving to Shannon Airport, I was confident that all would be well. Confidently and expectantly, I walked across the concourse towards the assembling group of my fellow travellers. As I did, a monstrous depression slammed down on my head and shoulders. It was as if some dark and heavy cloud had literally fallen on me.

In that instant, my interior world altered. The brightness and excitement of my anticipation were replaced by dread and

47

darkening gloom. The pain of depression returned. Somehow I gathered myself together and, resuming my actor's role, sat awaiting the plane's take-off. I was committed whether I liked it or not. Strapped into my seat, I weighed up my options and was immensely disappointed. One possibility lay in taking the first return flight back to Cork, but to have done so would have meant exposing my illness to the very people from whom I wished to conceal its existence.

Gradually I settled into my reliable coping mode. By the grace of God, I survived the subsequent days and the various events and encounters in San Francisco. While I was there, my vital medications were stolen from my hotel bedroom. It took urgent persuasion to obtain their replacement. What had promised to be a pleasant respite became quite the opposite.

About that time, yet another new and surreal imagery conjured itself up in my mind. It was manifested as if I were trekking through a deep canyon. It was an involuntary imaging, and startlingly realistic. Either I was slip-sliding down a narrow and steep dusty track into the depths of the arid canyon or alternatively I was struggling upwards seeking a beckoning comfort zone higher up.

When I did descend to the floor of this imaginary canyon, I experienced a reassuring sense of comfort. It wasn't possible to descend deeper. My symptoms were not going to become worse. I had literally reached 'rock bottom'. Descent implied a worsening of my symptoms. As I trudged along at the lowest level of the dusty track, my depression stabilised, settling itself comfortably on my shoulders, inside a metaphorical backpack. In this imaginary state, life was bearable and predictable. I sensed a measure of control. Things were not going to deteriorate. Once on the floor of the canyon, I knew that I would be able to endure and cope, whatever the future might throw up. I've no recall of how long this strange experience lasted. One day it simply ceased. I had never visited a canyon that resembled it remotely.

Throughout the depression, I used to judge my medications by their side-effects. Some were far more intrusive than others. All induced a persistent and unpleasant chemical taste in my mouth. Each had to be evaluated carefully in relation to my diet. There were various constraints. Cheese, which I dearly loved, was frequently a hazard. Alcohol was invariably forbidden. This latter wasn't a problem as I drank very little and infrequently. I had learned early on that alcohol was a depressant, and had suffered accordingly.

I remember one new medication. My psychiatrist was optimistic about its prospects. Nevertheless it caused me to walk with a leftward bias. It was puzzlingly awkward. Consciously, and repeatedly, I corrected my direction. At the same time, I developed a tremor in my hands, which made drinking difficult. Later again, and even more disturbingly, I lost my signature. I had to practise it as often as thirty-eight times — the number of lines on a page — before I could pen a convincing signature. At the first opportunity, I described these effects to my psychiatrist. He threw up his hands in alarm and switched me to a different drug.

I recall, in the latter stages of my illness, travelling by plane to Manchester Airport. For some unknown reason, this severe phase of my illness was punctuated by brief periods of relative comfort. In this instance, I was meeting pleasant people in order to wind up an engineering collaboration that had run its useful course. Stress was not in prospect. I had finished my breakfast and was admiring the sunlit clouds far below and the limitless blue skies overhead. Flying had held my interest since boyhood and remained a source of joyful escape. The mechanics, speed and dynamics of flying fascinated me, as they do to this day.

Without notice, my sense of inner comfort was dispersed and replaced by a dark depression. In concert, my vision shifted laterally as dysfunctional black-and-white television screens used to do in the past. My vision also acquired a shifting frame. Whatever I saw, I viewed it between the confines of this dark surround. Horrified at the prospect of the imminent meeting and its potential for exposure, I frantically sought escape. On reflection, I realised that there was none. I had to face the meeting. In the taxi, I wrestled with my inner self, striving to control my thoughts and eyesight. At the office venue, the entrance door eerily shifted laterally.

Fortunately I was meeting an affable and talkative group. Once engaged in the discussion, I regained control. The business was speedily attended to and signed off, and we settled into a vinous and chatty lunch. I coped very well throughout and made it back to the plane in one piece. I was hugely relieved as the accelerating plane pressed the seat firmly against my back: I had survived the day. Nevertheless I was troubled. I wondered what would happen next.

X

I use the term *demons of depression* in attempting to describe my mental experiences of the abstract intellectual and spontaneous symptoms of my depression. Other authors use it, too. It's an apt phrase in describing many of the inner occurrences that I experienced. In those tortured years, it seemed to me that my mind was, as it were, utterly crowded by most unpleasant and deeply disturbing occupants. They were torturing my imagination. They caused me immense distress. A demon is a supernatural being which is, at the same time, 'cruel, malignant, destructive and fierce'. I identified numerous such lodgers in my mind. I didn't associate these demons with

Satan. They were apart from religion. They were no more than the imaginative manifestations of my depression, but they hurt and at times struck terror on my inner being. I can clearly recall, in the days immediately following my cure, searching for them in the innermost recesses of my mind. Magically, they had disappeared. In their place, I experienced a cool peacefulness enveloping my entire mind. It was a wonderful and an infinitely relieving sensation.

The demon fear came first in order of intrusiveness. It was overwhelmingly pervasive. It also had been the very first arrival, signalling the onset of depression. While it never went away, its intensity varied, as did its manner of assault. A constant state of fearfulness seemed to have attached itself permanently to my very nature. I lived in a pervasive fear of the unknown.

Pain followed on swiftly, the torturer supreme. Its nature altered from time to time. Sometimes it was just there, a vague, unwanted and distinctly uncomfortable presence, especially when it wasn't identified with a particular limb or organ. On its initial arrival, it was located in my midriff and stomach. At that stage, in the initial months of depression, its intensity was such that it all but paralysed my will to act or even to think. In the lattermost years, it lodged in my thighs, especially at evening time.

In and among these paining demons, anguish also resided from time to time, exerting its own particularly refinements. Anxiety and concern about the future mingled with guilt and a persistent morbidity of mind. I was perpetually anxious. Anxiety attached itself particularly to long-term tasks. It seemed to me that they would never be completed, when I invariably and desperately needed to complete them in the shortest possible time. Whenever I addressed a task that would necessarily endure far into the future, anxiety was there, hovering and winding me up into a more stressful state.

Worry was persistent company. In good health, I'm a worrier and have always been so. Some of my worrying was constructive, however. It often converted itself to useful and positive anticipations. Arising from my depression, my worries were exaggerated far beyond all reasonable proportions, though. They presented themselves as absolute impossibilities. Nevertheless, I continue to believe that a worrier operates at a higher level of alertness, always on the alert in anticipating matters that may be about to go wrong. However, in latter years I've come to appreciate that being a worrier is far from a good habit. It implies that I'm not a trustful person in a spiritual sense, that I lack faith. It signifies that I'm not truly committing both the past and the present to God. I'm now laboriously learning to live in the present and place my trust in God, the creator of all. With God alone, anything is possible.

As if I hadn't enough negativity, apprehensions unfailingly shuffled alongside. They, too, were exceedingly unwelcome. My apprehensive states were at their worst in the hours of darkness. Apprehensive imaginings camped on my mind, as I lay in bed in the darkness of night. Waking as I did between two and three o'clock in the morning, my mind had ample time to wilt under these assaults. As I lay there, these apprehensions marched across the horizon of my mind, frequently appearing as an unending range of high and impassable mountains, rearing tall, dark and intimidating above the furthest horizon. There was no discernable route through them.

I became an insomniac early on in the life of the illness. Insomnia is typically a symptom of depression. At best, I was a poor sleeper. Habitual reading in bed from early boyhood didn't help. Possibly it was an unconscious form of escape. Inevitably it ate into my hours of sleep. Quite often, I would read two books concurrently, switching from one to the other as the mood took me. I enjoyed literary fiction immensely. I loved it. Non-fiction, travel, religion, biographies, psychology and certain technical topics like management attracted me also. I found it difficult to put down a book once my attention was engaged. There were times, in my teens, when I read under the blankets with the aid of a bicycle lamp, so pressing was the content of a book.

Consequently and well before the depression arrived I was missing out on an hour or two of sleep, possibly even more on occasions. Regrettably this habit became deep-seated, and by the time I had reached my twenties, it was causing daytime spells of drowsiness. I now believe that the depression climbed in on this. The illness permitted a mere three or four hours of sleep, and the consequent waking hours were distressing. The demons of my illness took over during the night hours. Sleeping tablets were ineffective in the longer term, and I had to devise my own remedies.

My sleepless hours, among other distractions, were frequently dominated by apprehensions relating to the immediate future. As each negative possibility grasped the attention of my mind, it expanded its negative potential. These possibilities never failed to loom worse and worse, no matter how forcefully I endeavoured to inject a positive spin. They fed on my imagination, which leant towards the pessimistic.

At some point during those terrible years, I noticed how the worse my apprehensions became, the realities of the following day were never anything as bad as my distorted imagination suggested. Grasping on to this in later years, I began deliberately to wind myself up with the very worst of possible apprehensions. Eventually this contorted practice of fooling myself, as it were, actually reduced the worst from my negative night dreams. My sleepless hours even diminished somewhat. The subsequent work hours were pleasant.

I can't recall what prompted me, but when in bed I used

to practise relaxing my leg muscles in a carefully measured progression from my feet upwards. Commencing with the toes, I would visualise each bone joint in my feet being pulled apart ever so gently, thereby permitting the bones to relax and to move fractionally apart from their neighbours. I visualised each bone floating free of the adjoining one. I would work on every bone from the tip of each toe until they all became suspended in a lethargic relaxation. For the ankles, I visualised a point of intense light working its way swiftly in and around and across the complexities of the ankle bones and tendons, relaxing all that it passed over or in between. A most definite sensation of relaxation accompanied each step in this mental progression. I suppose it was an intuitive form of autosuggestion.

Following on, I would concentrate on the leg muscles as far as the knee. I would commence with the muscles close to the shin bone, visualising them being physically, as it were, eased gently apart and smoothed into a state of somnolent relaxation. It wasn't quite an imaginary kneading and teasing out of the muscles, but something very close to it. As I mentally worked the shin and calf muscles in the same manner, I sensed each of them easing into a state of languorous twitching ease. As this state established itself, I used to wonder if it could be measured or assessed by some electronic medical process.

My knees were treated in the same manner as the ankles. The imaginary point of intense light raced in and about the joint and under the kneecap, spreading relaxation in its wake. From there I moved on to the big thigh muscles until all of my legs felt as once they had during teenage reluctant morning awakenings; so languorous were my limbs that I hadn't the slightest inclination to move my legs.

I rarely got beyond halfway up my thighs before sleep overwhelmed me. I have no idea how long I practised this intellectual soporific, but it certainly worked successfully for many years. Sadly the worsening symptoms of depression defeated it and eventually I simply couldn't mobilise the will to practise this routine.

From there on, I resorted to exercising on the floor. I discovered that by performing certain callisthenics, including squats, press-ups, abdominal exercises and others, until I was panting, beneficial effects were mobilised. I would get into bed immediately on completing the routine. By the time my breathing had subsided from panting to its normal rest rate, I would experience a comparable state of languor to the leg relaxation. This would spread throughout my entire physical being, and sleep followed rapidly. If it didn't, I would get out of bed and repeat the exercises. If I awoke from sleep, I would do the same thing. I still practise this today, and it continues to be effective.

The intellectual inertia that characterised my depression caused me endless frustrations. Even when I knew that certain things had to be done immediately, this negative constraining force too often prevented me from making an instant start. I had to haul myself, both mentally and physically, into commencing a task. All obligatory undertakings were affected similarly, from the largest to the smallest. I know that it isn't easy to associate a brake with a demon, but this particular kind of obstruction was truly demonic.

Restlessness also afflicted me. I had no sooner arrived in one place than I felt a simmering urge to be off to the next appointment on my schedule. It was difficult for me to sit still. Despite myself, there was a need to rush, rush, rush onwards to the unending tasks ahead in the false hope that I might get everything done now, and out of the way. Even while occupied on a long-enduring task at my desk, part of my mind was restlessly straining to complete it soonest so that I could move on. This, paradoxically, was in conflict with the pervasive inertia that dogged my waking hours. I was trapped between the two. In its own way, it helped me to meet the unyielding deadlines that often characterised my work commitments. But it bred an unwelcome and complex inner urgency.

Insecurity encompassed my spirit. In my furthest recall, I felt insecure. Depression wound up this aspect of my nature. I did daily battle with this scourge. I strove to be positive, to attain faith and self-belief through prayer and the incessant reading and study of inspirational books. Maybe reality lay in the fact that I wasn't truly grounded in a spiritual sense. My self-centring processes had been knocked askew by the assaults of this doleful illness. Depression fed on this. It worked against my efforts to move into the positive. It undermined my self-respect, any residual self-esteem and my self-confidence. I failed to love myself.

It was painfully obvious to me that, as a depressive, I was different from all those around me. I realised that I was no longer like my friends and colleagues. I realised that I was no longer capable of relating readily to others, even to my closest friends. A perpetual and invisible barrier imposed itself between us. A sense of aloneness, or isolation, affected me subtly. I lived in sharp isolation from those who enjoyed good health. They, on their side of the divide, had no idea where I dwelt, even as I chatted to them. They couldn't even begin to appreciate the extent of my utter detachment from the normality of their world. There were times when it was abundantly clear to me that I was entirely on my own.

Somehow, I had to find my solitary way through life, and onwards towards my destiny, by maintaining my belief in my intuitive reasoning. Suffering can and does concentrate the mind on negative possibilities. Depression, for the most part, emphasised my aloneness. Recognition that I had become a solitary being became part of my life and thought processes.

Those who are fatally ill must feel very much alone.

A sense of being a captive intruded persistently on my sensibilities for a very long period during the middle years of the illness. One day, it occurred to me that I was indeed a prisoner, but one detained behind invisible walls. In real terms, of course, I was a captive to my incurable depression, and it seemed that there would be no escape ever. So strong was this feeling that I used the title *Invisible Hostage* as my working title for this book.

Elsewhere I have described the extraordinary internal symptoms that seemed, forcefully to me at least, to be clearly visible to others in my immediate presence. They weren't, of course. To a large extent, these affected my vision, as I've explained earlier. They, in particular, made me feel a bizarre oddity, a person wholly apart. In this same context, I was also affected by this tantalising sense of otherness. Truly, I felt a difference that I couldn't escape. In another way, I lived outside the boundary of the normality of life, invariably an onlooker. There was another demonic phase that escapes detailed recall. It was nightmarish in its detail and intruded itself even when I was fully engaged with another. It affected my imagination, contorting it extraordinarily with uncomfortable visions that I couldn't disperse.

Tension was yet another symptom. From an early stage, I had become a tense person. This inner tension was the most obvious of my symptoms. A few kindly souls remarked on it. It wasn't always possible to conceal it; it showed itself on my drawn features.

Finally, I suffered from an edginess of spirit. My nerves were all too often on edge. This meant that I was irritable, an irritability that I find difficult to comprehend today. Of course, irascibility climbed in on this overall act, despite my belief that I was unable to become angry.

All of these demons combined to make my life extraordinarily difficult. I'm not at all clear just how I managed to cope between these states and the more familiar medical symptoms. The grace of God most certainly played a vital part in my survival. I unquestionably accept this. Otherwise I wouldn't have kept going. I fall back on St Paul's statement: 'It is when I am weak that I am strong.'

To a limited extent, I have now captured certain of these demons in print. I knew that they existed in the plural, but not that they amounted to quite as many as I have recorded. Considerable time elapsed before I could put verbal shapes upon them. I hope that my efforts to describe them may be a source of understanding and maybe even consolation to those currently struggling with depression. They are not alone in their tribulations and hugely strained feelings. Don't give up your struggles to cope and to appear normal. Countless other anonymous beings have done it, and are doing just that today and at this very moment. You can and you will do it. 'Be brave and great forces will come to your aid.' 'You are stronger than you think.' 'Everything is possible with God.' 'Trust in the Lord with all thy heart and lean not on thy own understanding.' These quotations genuinely inspired me, and continue to do so today.

XI

Despite the disturbing incidents I have described, other and better things were happening. On the suggestion of a friend, I visited an intercessor who had given up two successful and well-paying careers to concentrate on asking God to help others. He was tall and handsome and exuded self-confidence. His voice was deeply resonant. He listened carefully to my story, studying me as I spoke.

'Do you ask God to change those people who seem to trouble you a lot?' he asked when I had finished. I had been relating some of the challenges of my working life.

'I suppose I do,' I answered.

'Even if God did change them, you know, the outcome might not suit you at all,' he suggested. 'You might very well dislike the altered personality. Instead, I suggest your prayers should go something like this: "I praise you, Lord, in Sean as he is, God bless him and change me."' He looked at me and asked, 'Do you understand?'

'Never thought of it that way,' I replied, having instantly appreciated the inherent charity and common sense of this prayer. I realised that it would be far more appropriate if I were the one to be changed. There and then I adopted this particular prayer, and I continue to recite it to this day.

'Do you thank God in anticipation when you ask Him for a favour?' he continued, studying me. 'Don't you think that you should?'

I paused, holding his gaze. 'Yes, I suppose I should, now that you raise the question. I hadn't thought about God in that way. Yes, I see that I should be grateful in anticipation, if I genuinely believe that He is going to help me.'

We chatted on for a while.

Abruptly he turned to me. 'Now we'll see if we can work a miracle. Put your left leg up there, that's it, on my knee. I know that you have a problem here.' He prayed out loud over my leg while I distractedly wondered how on earth he could have known about my pain. I hadn't a limp or any visible constraint that I had ever noticed. There was a recurring dull pain above my left hip, nothing else.

Sadly there was no miracle. Later it occurred to me that it was I who didn't believe that one was going to happen. I was certainly taken by surprise when the possibility of a miracle was mentioned and maybe my reaction was too slow. Whichever, the dull pain remained.

He went on to explain that whenever he needed money it invariably arrived — that is, whenever he and his family had a genuine shortfall. 'One evening, my wife and I and our children sat down at the table for our evening meal. Unspeaking, we each realised that there was absolutely no food in the house. We sat silently staring at one another. While this pause persisted, I thought that I heard a sound at the hall door. I went out and opened it. There was a large brown paper parcel on the doorstep. Picking it up, I could feel that it was hot. Puzzled, I looked up and down the road. There were neither people nor traffic about. Inside the paper was a large piping-hot meat pie. That's the kind of thing that happens.' He smiled engagingly.

I departed from that marvellously confident man in a more hopeful frame of mind. I sensed the depth of his faith and marvelled at it. I deeply regretted my inability to believe that he was going to cure the pain in my lower back.

There were three other curious incidents, spaced widely apart, during those very worst years. They still intrigue. The first was late on a November Saturday afternoon. Golfing, I was walking downhill toward the fourteenth green, close to the clubhouse. There had been nothing remarkable about either the company or the events of that day. Of a sudden, my depression dispersed. In a millisecond, it was gone. Every single one of the torturing and angst-ridden symptoms disappeared. The grass of the course was a brighter and richer green. The low clouds had a lighter tone of grey. I didn't know what to think. It had happened so suddenly, I was confounded. I was entirely at peace with myself. Suddenly I loved my golfing companions. I said nothing to them about this extraordinary experience. It would have taken too long even to begin to explain it and its implications. We played on and finished our game. I don't remember anything further, other than that I sat down to tea and toast, having changed.

This 'window' in my illness lasted maybe three hours or so. I can't be certain. I've since failed to find an explanation. Within that brief spell, I wasn't able to get my mind around what had happened to me. How could such a profound change take place within me and in such a short time? How could my physical and mental being alter with such extraordinary rapidity? Was it an instance of spontaneous interactions between as-yet-unknown internal healing substances? It certainly happened. There's absolutely no doubt in my mind that the depression lifted. Was it another instance of divine intervention? I still wonder.

Perhaps two years later, I was following, on foot, a beagle pack hunting a hare. It was wintertime. Just as before, the depression vanished in all of its symptoms. It was gone for the second time. There hadn't been the slightest warning. What power had dispersed the complex symptoms of my illness so swiftly? Years later, I still haven't found an answer. I failed to record the duration of this second 'window' also. In time, I interpreted these two brief 'windows' as hopeful signposts for the future.

Some years later again, I was in Switzerland, sitting in a mountain train as it climbed steeply upwards on rails that wound their way through fresh snowfields. It was early morning. A brilliant sun sparkled on innumerable snowflakes lying on the rounded contours of the night's snowfall. Tall snow-capped peaks reached up into a blue sky. Across the precipitous valley, peak after majestic peak reared skywards, one above the other. As it always did, the Matterhorn drew my eyes to its elegantly sculpted profile, permanently pointing skywards. On that morning, it was truly majestic. My fellow passengers spoke to one another in mid-European languages that I didn't understand.

Then it happened. The depression vanished. It absolutely lifted. Instantly I loved everyone in the carriage. I was at peace and intensely happy. The pain and the demons of my depression vanished. The stupendous alpine scenery outside the carriage windows was both closer to me and more beautiful than I had ever experienced it previously. The reflected sunlight on the snow sparkled with an intensely white brilliance.

This 'window' seemed to have lasted longer than on previous occasions. I was so bemused that I didn't tell my ski companions when I rejoined them later. There was an instinctive privacy about these experiences. In any event, my mind was totally preoccupied by the exquisite inner peace and joy that I was experiencing. It was bliss on a grand scale. None of my companions, who were well known to me, commented on my bearing. What I saw and experienced was concealed from them. Regrettably it was to be the final 'window'. Together, however, these 'windows' engendered in me a new, silent and unspoken hopefulness for the future.

In retrospect, it is difficult to place these extraordinary occurrences in any particular perspective. My psychiatrist took little interest in them. Nevertheless, they remain sharp and clear in my memory: intense highlights in a darkened and painful passage of my life.

XII

Life progressed despite the mounting intensity of my sufferings. A colleague and I facilitated a meeting between a friend who was ill and a healing priest from England. Afterwards it struck me that I should have spoken to this priest about my problems. Fired by desperation, I called him on the phone. Initially he explained his inability to meet me: he was very busy, he said. Somehow, in my anxiety, I prevailed on him, not appreciating at that time just how busy a parish priest could be. Eventually he agreed to a meeting.

He made the arrangements. I was collected by a lady at Manchester Airport and brought to her elegant home in a quiet suburb. It was still early morning. She presented me with tea and toast and left me to do some paperwork. Several hours later, a tall priest raced up the open stairwell and literally bounded into the spacious living room. His powerful personality seemed to fill the tastefully furnished space. He smiled brilliantly and crushed my hand in his. Three young women followed almost immediately and later a lady, obviously in mourning, joined us. The priest was Monsignor Michael Buckley DD.

Throughout that entire day, this previously unknown group prayed over me with extraordinary fervour. Directed by Monsignor Buckley, they sang hymns, prayed aloud and laid their hands on my head and shoulders while they beseeched God to grant a cure for my depression. At Monsignor Buckley's request, I had brought with me a brief account of my life. He took it away to study when we broke for a light meal.

I became more and more uncomfortable as the day progressed. Eventually my embarrassment was genuinely acute. How was I going to repay these people? How could I adequately thank them? I hadn't expected anything like this. Why should they have taken so much trouble to pray for me, a total stranger? Some had travelled considerable distances. The praying continued well into the afternoon. Then Monsignor Buckley and I retired to another room, at his suggestion.

He tapped the sheets of paper with the back of his hand as he leant an elbow on the mantelpiece. On them was a brief résumé of my life. 'This is a terrible story,' he declared. 'It contains no hope; none whatsoever.' He went on questioning me. He walked across the room and then, returning to the mantelpiece, he turned to me. 'Your problem, Malachy, is that you've no faith. It's as simple as that.' He held my gaze unwaveringly.

Abashed, I couldn't deny his assertion. I was at the same time beginning to become angry at it, though. Fortunately my inner confusion silenced me. I don't remember the remainder of that afternoon, other than that the lady of the house provided us with yet another light meal. Afterwards I learned that they were members of a prayer group founded by Monsignor Buckley. That evening at the airport, he handed me a copy of one of his books. I read the title: *Why Are You Afraid?* 'Read that. It might help,' he said, smiling encouragingly, touching my shoulder in reassurance.

In the months that followed, I read and re-read the book, chapter by chapter, with a diligence and intensity that startled me. The appalling effects of my worsening depression were bearing down woefully on me. I was terrified at each new downturn. I sensed myself being nudged closer and closer to the ultimate abyss. Terror coursed in my veins. Nevertheless, wounded as I was by Monsignor Buckley's unsought accusation, I began searching for an unambiguous definition of faith. As I did, it occurred to me that I didn't really under-stand the meaning of the word 'faith'. Eventually I accepted that I had been unthinkingly confusing faith itself with religion. I did eventually uncover the definition of faith.

XIII

The chronology of subsequent events is confused in my mind. The months and years staggered on their way as I struggled to cope with my responsibilities. Perhaps more than twenty years had passed when I began to discern changes in my beloved psychiatrist. He no longer was the competent and assured self whom I had known so well. Time and again, he seemed bothered when I called for my consultation. My file was sometimes missing.

I should here explain that his perusal of his notes during consultations was, for me, the high point of the ritual of our encounters. It indicated to me the depth of his interest in and concern for my welfare. As he perused his notes of our previous consultation, I sat on the edge of my chair in high expectation, willing him to find good news. Invariably there was none. Nevertheless, stubbornly I continued to hope.

At a subsequent consultation and before he had said anything, he stood up abruptly from his desk and, turning, he walked across the room to the window directly facing his desk. Turning back towards me, he raised his hands high above his head. 'How do you do it, Malachy? You continue to live and work as a useful citizen. Don't you know that only two per cent of depressives cope with depression as severe as yours is. Yet you manage to endure it and somehow cope usefully with life? The remainder of people in your situation, the other ninety-eight per cent, go under. How do you do it?' He dropped his hands and returned, slightly embarrassed, to his seat.

Afterwards, when I had time to digest the implications of his questioning, I was heartened by his extraordinary and wholly uncharacteristic outburst. He was an undemonstrative man, as I had long previously learned. His words clearly suggested that my struggle was an unusual one, and that I had become one of a small and unique band of two per cent of all depressives. Clearly he was impressed by my tenacity. Up to that point, I hadn't thought anything of my efforts other than their obvious ineffectiveness. As far as I was concerned, I simply had to keep going. There was nothing more to it; neither was there any choice. I had to accept my lot and get on with life as best I could. I was greatly encouraged and warmed by this unexpected insight.

Some time later, while writing a motoring article on a typical winter Saturday afternoon in my home, uncharacteristically I was labouring unduly at this familiar and normally enjoyable task. I just couldn't find the right words or expressions. This was unusual. It was a puzzlingly obstinate difficulty. I had always enjoyed writing, an activity that invariably came easily to me. Now I was baulked. I was perplexed.

The very next instant, my mind was entirely taken up with suicide, my suicide. There were no introductory thoughts. One moment I was searching for ideas and words; the next I was planning my demise. Without any prior consideration, I accepted the fact of my utter worthlessness. This came from nowhere. There was no lead-in. My new sense of worthlessness was such that I felt of absolutely no use or value to anyone, including my wife and family. There was no doubt about this in my mind. I was totally convinced that my death would be the only source of release for my family and myself.

These unexpected suicidal thoughts were bewildering. They progressed to feelings of utter self-rejection Everyone close to me, I was convinced, would be far better off if I were to put myself entirely out of their way. I went on to consider which kind of death would be quickest and least painful. Yes, death had to be the answer to my unrelenting and ever-intensifying suffering, twenty years and more of it. Suddenly I realised that I couldn't take it any more. One moment, my writing task fully occupied my mind; the next moment, plans for my suicide were overwhelmingly present.

This radically negative view of life caused me neither bewilderment nor fear, not even disturbance or worry. I accepted it unquestioningly. It wasn't just a view; it was a deep conviction. Coolly and calmly I observed myself planning my annihilation. Yet an observing part of me couldn't believe it, that another part of self was doing just that. I was conscious of being both observer and the observed at one and the same time. Within days, I had reached a decision on the means of my exiting this mortal world. I would crash my car at high speed into a disused bridge abutment. I knew the bridge, the precise location of the point of impact, and positively appreciated the added benefit of the straight downhill approach.

For the next few weeks, my mind swung between this vast compulsion to kill myself, and the opposing moral and practical arguments against doing so. These latter had been evolving in counterpoint. God would never wish me to kill myself, I kept reminding my reasoning self. He forbade murder and by implication self-destruction. Self-murder had to be a worse moral offence, in my judgment. To commit it would be a mortal sin. My immortal soul would go to hell for all eternity. I repeatedly reminded myself of this. I unreservedly believed this.

It didn't occur to me to evaluate my objectivity. Neither did it occur to me to discuss my suicidal tendency with anyone other than my psychiatrist. As it happened, he did ask me if I was suicidal at that particular time. When I confirmed that I was, he didn't remark on it; he looked at me for some moments and then moved on to another point. His lack of comment still puzzles. Possibly he knew that I wasn't the type who would commit suicide.

Then one morning, on waking, I had a vision of the utter devastation that would descend on my family in the aftermath of my suicide. I recalled suicides in families I knew. This realisation proved to be the turning point. The compulsion remained, but now it was possible to nudge it aside. I knew by then that I wasn't going to do it. Yet the persuasive suicidal compulsion persisted for several weeks. Eventually the episode passed.

Two more identical suicidal states followed in succession, possibly several weeks apart, but each subsequent episode was a shade easier to deal with, having survived the initial on-slaught. In time, their passing reassuringly highlighted the fact that my suicidal tendencies had vanished. In my instance, the suicidal compulsions didn't last. They were passing experiences.

XIV

A bright spark of relief during those sombre winters was my skiing break in the Alps. Initially my reaction to this holiday all but transcended my depression. I was uplifted by the reality of being in contact with snow and experiencing the effects of high altitude. I appreciated the thin dry air. My normally strong hair became soft and controllable. The up-lighting effect of reflected light altered people's appearances. The combined effect of these injected a measure of joy in my being. The intense sunlight bouncing off the snow and the magnificence of the surrounding snow-capped peaks inspired me.

I recall one occasion, in early times, being so uplifted, energised and replete with confidence and energy that I couldn't wait to return to my office desk. The brilliant light and the joy of skiing combined to transport me from my melancholic mood to higher emotions. In later times, the delights arising from skiing failed to compare in any way with that particular visit. While I loved the ambience and exulted in the skiing, the depression adhered to my being. I could do nothing about it, other than pray.

The skiing brought its exultation especially when I completed a challenging run. In terms of distraction from depression, the intellectual demands of skiing at speed required the entire focus of my mind on staying upright and successfully executing each turn or shift in direction. My mind had to keep pace with the snow that raced up to the tips of my skis. Each and every variation of the snow's surface had to be identified and awarded the appropriate response. These occurred instant by instant, placing such urgent demands on my reactions that together they entirely concentrated the focus of my mind. This speed and level of attention hauled my mind into the present moment, as it strained to keep pace with the demands of remaining upright despite the hazards rushing at my skis. It reminded me of driving at high speed on a testing race circuit. The demands were similar. The passage of time seemed to be suspended. I lived in the present while on skis. In those fleeting downhill passages I had all that I desired in life.

On one of these visits to my favourite resort, Zermatt in Switzerland, I was absorbed in reading and re-reading Monsignor Buckley's book, *Why Are You Afraid?* On returning to my hotel each afternoon, I retired to bed and concentrated on the particular day's reading. This had been going on for months. Unknown to myself, it was, in retrospect, a form of reading meditation. So my psychiatrist commented later when I told him of this practice. He both encouraged and approved of it.

On some later occasion, possibly shortly after a ski vacation, the contents of that slim book resolved themselves into a spontaneous and silent mantra, 'Jesus loves me, Jesus loves me, Jesus loves me,' which repeated and repeated itself silently in my mind. I found it difficult to believe that it was happening. On and on it continued of its own volition from the moment of awakening each morning. The recitation persisted silently all day, other than when I was entirely engaged with others at work or on a pressing task. This spontaneous praying lasted for several weeks. I can't be certain just how long it continued.

Then, with the same abruptness of its arrival, it ceased. Instantly I was lifted into a wondrous, blissfully happy and joyous state on a sunlit plateau. This indescribable experience was to last all of six weeks. Suddenly I loved everyone around me, even those who had frequently troubled me. I became hugely tolerant. My shyness disappeared. I loved my wife in a manner I had never experienced before. I became gregarious. At a party, I was asked to sing. Having no voice, I was invariably embarrassed by such a request. On this occasion, however, I bounced up on my feet and made an inconsequential, humorous and teasing speech.

Time raced by in a marvellous succession of positive and constructive reactions. Work-related challenges all but resolved themselves while I was living in a blissful state. No matter what situations demanded, I remained rational and in control of my thoughts and responses. No one remarked on my good humour or questioned my altered mood although I must have seemed a different person. Even my wife didn't comment during that spell! I still don't understand these happenings other than to accept them humbly as incidents of divine intervention. It had to be noticeable to others, I reasoned. Or perhaps this gifted state was solely for the pleasure of my innermost self. I don't know. I have never experienced such happiness either before or since.

Inevitably and abruptly, this other-than-life existence unravelled along its edges. It was like a cloud beginning to shred itself at its perimeter. Panicking at the prospect of losing this happy state, I began reciting the mantra frantically, 'Jesus loves me; Jesus loves me; Jesus loves me,' in terrified desperation. It was to no avail. Within a day, or maybe two, I was grounded, back on my mortal feet in my depressed, self-observing self.

XV

Within a year of the foregoing occurrences, I suffered three episodes of manic depression. While they were most disturbing, on the one hand, they were also stupendous in their vast surges of energy, both physical and intellectual.

Driving homewards across the city, on the return journey from a site visit, I had been motoring for several hours. It was evening time. I was impatiently anticipating being home and in the company of my wife, hungry for a meal and hoping for an evening of peaceful quietness. I was passing the entrance gates of the city graveyard where my parents are buried. My recall is vivid. Abruptly, the muscles on the back of my neck began relaxing one by one, entirely of their own volition. They seemed to slide one over another as if unravelling and adjusting themselves into a state of relaxation and comfort. Layer by layer, they slid and readjusted until all were comfortably loose. It was as dramatic as it was unexpected.

I had no idea what might have caused this phenomenon, having been told on several occasions that my neck muscles were abnormally stiff. I used to think that this was a consequence of supporting my large and characteristic family head. Otherwise, I felt that it was no more than a physical expression of my inner tension.

Within a day or two of this occurrence, my mental processes began to accelerate and race ahead at a furious rate. All sorts of marvellous ideas streamed across my mind. My work rate accelerated in parallel. I was ready to tackle any task. Part of the gloom of my days was sidelined by the excitement of solving this or that challenge.

Apprehensions vanished — well, most of them. I grasped at opportunities the instant they occurred to me. I was elated. Elation had released the inertial brakes on my will. It took some time before I comprehended all that was happening to me, and came to terms with this new and extraordinary experience.

I recall little else of the detail of the initial episode of manic depression. I do, however, remember contacting a cousin who held a very senior position in a large business in Dublin. I had come across what I believed to be a marvellous means of promoting his firm's activities. It was being used in one or two places in Europe. My cousin was very polite. 'I'll think about it,' he said. The idea, of course, implied exciting construction implications. I had a vision of an intriguing design challenge, not to mention badly needed fees.

When I looked back on that call afterwards, I winced. Today I manage to smile at that uncharacteristic initiative. My approach was extremely naive: far too direct. Later, I learned that such an initiative was classically symptomatic of manic depression. During the three episodes of this vastly and paradoxically energising version of depression, it was the sole occasion when I potentially wrong-footed myself seriously.

The strange thing about this variant of depression is the fact that I still remained depressed, even though I was enjoying enormous physical and intellectual strength. Paradoxically the vast energies available in this manic state conflicted with the relentlessly downbeat and ever-restraining depression. The downside lies in the reality of an unrelenting need to be doing and doing and doing. There was no rest and certainly no relaxation. It was a state of untiring restlessness. I don't remember how long that initial episode endured.

I have little recall of the second episode. I do remember that I kept a close watch on myself and on any erupting initiatives. I'm surprised that I have no recall of my accelerated work rate during that particular episode. However, I have clear recall of the third episode. Aware of what was taking place, I monitored my actions carefully. There was no misstep this time.

I was extremely busy at the time and got on with my work in what I believed to be a reasonable and efficient manner. One day, I handed a dictation tape to my secretary. She stared at me, eyebrows raised. 'But, you've given me two tapes already today. What's happening?' She laughed.

I had absolutely no idea that I was dictating coherently at such rapidity. My secretary was well aware of my normal productivity, and I was startled by her comment. Observing myself closely, I began to appreciate that I was sweeping through my work at an astonishing pace. There was little conscious effort involved. Indeed, the fact that I remained oblivious to my hugely increased productivity was indicative of the power of the surge of energy in my system.

Domestically, I don't remember any undue incident. Things between my wife and me must have been somewhat easier. I'm certain that I was more talkative and possibly more assertive.

In terms of physical energy and available strength, this manic depression levelled all the inclines on my hilly running circuit. It was an extraordinary sensation, running uphill without any effort whatsoever. Invariably each rise normally presented me with a stern physical challenge. I didn't relish their approach. Yet there I was, soaring up and over them, as if they didn't exist. During the episodes, getting up in the mornings was not a problem either. In my enhanced energies, I all but bounced out of my bed.

Despite this, the experience was not a pleasant one. I became a driven person. Relaxation was impossible. I lived in a state of tireless exhaustion.

Kay Redfield Jamison provides a vivid and dramatic account of her struggles with manic depression in her book, *An Unquiet Mind*. It is a fascinating book in many ways. Wonderfully written, it provides a startling insight into the problems of the mania that can attach itself to depression. Recounting one particular incident, she describes how she and a medical colleague were running circuits around the hospital car park in the dark hours of early morning — she was a psychiatrist and was endeavouring to tire herself in the hope of finding sleep. A police car drew up and enquired what on earth they were doing. It took some persuading to convince the police that they were both doctors from the nearby medical centre and that she needed to tire herself in the hope of a night's sleep!

Between her manic episodes, she was unable to function. She sat at her desk, staring out the window, awaiting the arrival of the next manic surge. In comparison to hers, my manic episodes were mild.

The episodes were extremely interesting but I wouldn't wish to experience them again. It is a complex condition and I know that I have failed to describe it adequately. It is difficult to imagine where the energy comes from. It was vast and relentless.

XVI

Towards the end of that bewildering manic period, twice I had to beat a retreat to St Edmundsbury, the convalescent home I had come to love. The sheer intensity of the physical pain and the torturing of the demons of depression became altogether too much. I couldn't take any more. I desperately needed a respite. I hadn't passed through its gates for twenty years, but I fled there in search of comforting relief.

I spent two fortnights there. On both occasions, I was suspended under the effects of narcosis for the first week. When I first came to, I was bewildered. Realising that a week had elapsed, I had no recall of anything within its days. Apparently

I had spent that same week walking about in the home, affably chatting to anyone I met. But I hadn't the slightest recollection of those conversations or encounters. It was as if an entire week had been wiped out of my mind.

On both of the subsequent weeks, I was fully conscious and feeling surprisingly good. I checked and re-checked with the patients to whom I had spoken while under narcosis. 'Yes, you chatted away to me,' was the invariable response. 'You were in great form.' At the end of both second weeks I was discharged, feeling ready to cope with the bigger world. However, these dramatic improvements didn't endure. The depression reasserted itself within three weeks or so of discharge. Nevertheless, I managed to cope for a significant period following the second discharge.

My depression, at that stage, was spiralling downwards at an awesome rate. The dreaded ever-threatening chasm was edging close. While my mind rejected the notion of death, pessimistically I had concluded that I could well be retired to a mental home. That was my bleakest prospect. I dreaded it.

At the next consultation, my psychiatrist was obviously unwell. He was not himself. He seemed bothered and disturbed. There were shadows under his eyes. By then, we had been meeting every three months for almost twenty years, and we had both aged in the process, I reminded myself. He didn't smile when I entered his room, but looked at me from under his eyebrows. His manner was uncharacteristically abrupt. 'There's nothing further that I can do for you, I'm afraid, Malachy; it's up to you now,' he said, or words to that effect. I was stunned into silence and said very little as the dread import of his words sank into my mind. I discovered later that he had conveyed the very same message to my wife over the telephone. She was furious with him.

This did not help. The depression plunged deeper.

Inevitably I was unable to work. Steeling myself to tell my colleagues that I would have to retire, I procrastinated. I did succeed in clearing my desk preparatory to my departure. In the meantime, anxiously checking my financial affairs with an accountant, I found that my material circumstances were insecure. There were still eight years to elapse before my pension matured. In my downcast judgment, my situation was hopeless. I didn't know what to do or where to turn.

On one occasion within that doom-laden phase, I was at a party in a friend's house. I avoided parties as much as possible but I was pleasantly surprised, on this evening, at being at my ease and actually enjoying myself. I recall standing alone, observing, listening and watching the interplay of personalities around me. From nowhere, it seemed, I noticed a lady walking purposefully across the room in my direction. I didn't know her well. I knew her husband better: we had been in the same school. She was, in my estimation, a shy person and invariably wore dark glasses on social occasions. She stopped directly in front of me. 'I know that you're a depressive,' she said. 'I was a depressive. I know someone who could do something for you. I want to talk to you in private.' It was a demand rather than a polite request. Her directness was intimidating.

Failing to find a quiet space in the crowded house, we eventually sat on the stairs. She explained how an acupuncturist had cured her depression. As she spoke, guests squeezed past us on trips to the toilet. 'You must go to him,' she said. She was very insistent. Pausing, she handed me a slip of paper. 'This is his phone number and address. It's easy to find. Do go to him.'

In bed that night, I rejected her suggestion. It reeked of voodoo or some jungle medicine. I knew absolutely nothing about acupuncture. Anyway, my loyalties lay with my doctors and my psychiatrist, I told myself.

Yet within that same week, I was standing at the door of

that acupuncturist's shabby cottage clinic, utterly panic-stricken. Within that time, my depression had plunged further to new and terrifying depths. I wasn't thinking clearly. I just had to find a cure, anywhere, anyhow. Terror had frozen my mind.

XVII

Gerry Longfield, a slightly built man in a white coat, received me and welcomed me most cordially. His gold-rimmed glasses were unfashionably large. His fair hair was untidy. As I lay on an unusually tall couch, he questioned me in detail about my illness. He felt both pulses. As he did so, he moved his fingertips back and forth along the pulsing veins of each wrist.

He sat at the foot of the couch, his face at the same level as my feet. 'First, I'm going to treat you with reflexology,' he explained. While he spoke, he dusted his hands with white powder and commenced massaging my feet. 'I do this for diagnostic purposes,' he said. 'This is reflexology. Through it I learn the state of your major organs.' Then he proceeded to massage the sole of one foot with steely fingers. It really hurt in some areas. I writhed and exclaimed at each paining. He explained that particular locations in the soles of our feet are connected to the major body organs. The hurting signified problems within particular organs. 'This area pains because you are seriously stressed,' he said. He was working on the central area of the sole. 'Are you?' I nodded in affirmation.

'Right,' he exclaimed, having completed working over both feet. 'I'm moving on to acupuncture now.' Producing slender stainless steel needles, he proceeded to insert them at various points around the base of my right-hand thumb. Then he inserted more into my lower right leg and into my right foot. Almost every insertion induced a bolt of pain, just as an electric shock would. 'Good, good,' he murmured as I reacted to the discomfort. As he proceeded, he explained his purpose and the cause of my discomforts. 'I'm actually moving your Qi [chi],' he said.

When he had completed inserting the needles, he leant close to my ear. I was utterly bemused, yet disconcertingly relaxed. 'I think that I can do something for you,' he said. 'You have the heartbeat of an athlete. It's just great. I'll need to see you twice every week.' He stood back, regarding me.

Within a few weeks, I began to enjoy the company of this electrician-turned-acupuncturist. He was gifted with a sense of irony, a ready wit and humorous expression. He reminded me of several of my cycling companions of previous years. He was a true raconteur and possibly unaware of the extent of his gift. Throughout the treatments, between accounts of his own colourful past, he explained many aspects of Chinese medicine. The pain stemming from the insertion of the needles worsened as the treatments progressed. When I yelped, he simply responded, 'Good, good'.

The greater the hurt, the more effective the treatment, he explained. Frequently the insertion of the needles triggered a sensation as if invisible sparks streamed outwards from my fingertips or toes. I was intrigued. He had to be moving energy, I told myself. I would suffer the discomfort as long as I was convinced that this acupuncture was going to cure me, I decided. When I suggested that Qi was energy, just like electricity, he disagreed. 'It's Qi,' he insisted. We argued about this from time to time. I have since learned that Qi is a unique energy form. It's not electricity. Qi is slower.

Seven weeks later, I noticed subtle improvements in both my body and my mind following each treatment. These welcome respites unfortunately were followed by two-day regressions into an appalling level of depression. It became a three-steps-forward and two-steps-backwards progression. The pain of the insertion of the needles, followed by the regressions, eventually became too much for me. It was beyond my nervous reserves. I protested strenuously.

'Don't give up now, please don't,' he pleaded, his hands outspread. 'You're making real progress. I know. I can sense it. Please, please stay with it for your own sake. You'll be cured. I'm certain of this. Believe me. It's going to happen. You're going to be cured. Hang on, please!' His sincerity was undeniable. I appreciated that his persuasion was for my sake solely. 'You'll get better, I promise. Just hold on please.' He helped me off the couch.

'How long more? Can't you tell me? I'm not certain that I can take this for too long more,' I complained.

'Remember you've been ill for a long, long time. You can't expect to be cured in a short time. I know that you'll be cured. Try to be patient. I know that it isn't easy.'

And so I held on, enduring the discomforts reluctantly. Each evening following a treatment session, I fell into a deep sleep in an armchair, after our evening meal. This new sleeping pattern was untypical, insomniac as I was for many years. One evening, it was too much for my wife who became alarmed at this uncharacteristic behaviour. Vigorously she shook me awake. 'I thought that you were either dead or dying, your sleep was so deep and silent,' she said. She was pale with concern when I looked up at her.

XVIII

It was the tenth week of the treatment. I was sitting at the mealtime table, looking out on the blue sea below our cliff-side home. Unspeaking, I explored the innermost recesses of my mind. I was tentatively searching for the familiar turmoil of fear, pain, apprehension and restlessness, and even more so for the presence of the demons that had tormented me for so long. None of these symptoms was present. In their place, a peaceful and cooling stillness enveloped my mind. It seemed as if a cooling fluid was gently submerging my brain. It was a blissful sensation. I didn't wish either to move or to speak. On that particular day, I realised that the depression had gone. It was the very first time it had absented itself since its diagnosis twenty-five years earlier, with the exception of the three fleeting respite 'windows' of earlier years.

A new pattern developed. The depression would absent itself for a day at a time. Then it returned for two days only to disappear following each acupuncture treatment. I held on and observed. The depression-free spells gradually lengthened. Then the good days grew to become an entire week. My acupuncturist encouraged and reassured me: 'It will go. You're going to be well, and the depression won't come back. I know. That heartbeat of yours: it's great. I told you that I'd do something for you, didn't I? Do you remember? It'll be another while yet. Just keep coming. It's vital that you persist! When the depression does go, it will be gone for all time.'

Some weeks later, the depression had definitely vanished. The finality of its departure was anticlimactic, extremely private. I was afraid to accept the reality of a cure. It mightn't last. I had no inclination to talk to anyone, excepting my acupuncturist, about what was going on within myself. I had no inclination to reveal these changes to my long-suffering wife. There was no urge to jump about in exultation and celebration. I wasn't able to tell anyone about this for several weeks. I just couldn't bring myself to do this simple thing. I'm still uncertain why this was so. Perhaps the sheer profundity of the occasion shocked me into silence. Maybe my years of acting normally had built up a significant element of reserve within my nature. I can't be sure.

It was the profoundest of changes and I simply couldn't get my mind around it. Maybe this reluctance was an extension of my habitual silence in concealing my disease. Possibly it had become ingrained. Besides, I was bemused by people's apparent disinterest in my illness; even the medical practitioners whom I encountered from time to time showed no interest whenever I mentioned it.

Then a month or two later, my wife and I were enjoying a meal with old friends, a husband and wife. We had travelled to Kerry to meet them. 'I haven't had depression for two weeks now,' I announced spontaneously towards the end of the meal. I hadn't planned to make this statement. It was out.

'But your father had it. We all knew that,' my friend exclaimed after some moments of awkward silence. He and I had been at university together. My father was dean of the Faculty of Civil Engineering, which we both had attended. Startled, I stared at him. I had never known that my father had been a depressive. I had never even thought of him in that context. I was staggered by this insight.

I don't know whether or not my father ever recognised his illness for what it was. Did he just accept his inner suffering and diminishing intellectual energy as part of the life that had been presented to him at birth? Neither he nor my mother ever mentioned the word 'depression' in their sons' company. The fact that he suffered from angina was well known to us, though. We were fully aware of this and the medication that he swallowed every day. Did he, in genuine unawareness, decide to endure the appalling life as his inherited nature, and without the assistance of medications? It seems unlikely that he wouldn't have discussed it with a medical colleague in the university.

Decades later, I learned that his elder brother — my most generous godfather — had spent time in the Blarney Hydro being treated for depression. My genetic inheritance was beyond doubt.

Weeks passed. The depression didn't return. An egotistic sense of resentment gripped me; I was concerned that there hadn't been any excitement. Neither had there been any drama. I had anticipated wild urges to celebrate, yet I wasn't lifted out of myself by the merest suggestion of exultation. Yes, the depression was gone, but my day-to-day life was disappointingly banal: ordinary to say the least. It didn't seem right. I eventually realised that I was being woefully ungrateful. I should have been on my knees, giving thanks to a merciful and caring God. My prayers and those of my family and friends had been heard. God had moved the cure.

Nevertheless, I remained anxious about the stability of my healing. Would it endure? This was the pessimistic aspect of my nature. So many times while in the gloom of my illness, I had imagined what it might be like to experience life free of depression. I had even planned appropriate celebrations. Instead, my recovery was a non-event.

Common sense prevailed, and I accepted that I should be grateful to God, and to all those who had prayed for me. I was being selfish, I reprimanded myself. Still, something was missing. I was no more than my old flawed self. Surely the years of suffering should have wrought positive changes in my personality? After all those miserable years, it had come to just this! Even my willpower didn't seem to be stronger.

While striving to energise my will into action during the years of my depression, I used to fantasise that if ever my genuinely strengthened willpower were released from depression, I would be a marvel of instant action. It wasn't to be the case. When my unexpected and fortuitous cure did come about, and the 'brakes' of depression were released, I still had to address each new task consciously. However, doing so became vastly easier. The hoped-for flow of limitless unrestrained energy, conveying me effortlessly from one task to the next, didn't materialise. What I had been innocently daydreaming about was close to a manic release of relentless energy, such as I had experienced on the three occasions referred to earlier. This particular quality wasn't part of my nature, unfortunately.

Weeks slipped by. My productivity began to improve. I noticed people in the office studying me. My distracted wife observed me critically. I sensed her oblique scrutiny.

XIX

There was no warning. Abruptly everything changed: my entire inner being was lifted dizzily to unimaginably joyous heights. I soared ever so high, and even higher again, on a dizzying sky-borne euphoric trajectory. It was as if I had been transported up and away and ever so far away from my previous worldly troubles. I was replete with energy — a benign energising state of body and mind. The euphoria was vast. It was far beyond anything I might have imagined.

This was so different from events that had happened before. It was an out-of-this-world sensation. So high did I fly that the normal difficulties and challenges of life dwindled to become no more than minor tasks. I unravelled them effortlessly.

Anything and everything was possible. The metaphorical handbrake that had impeded my actions and reactions for so long had been disengaged. In its place an accelerator was available, just as I might need a surge of power to take action. All action was possible as soon as the very thought surfaced in my mind. Spontaneity replaced my laboured initiatives. At work, challenging issues no longer fazed me. Neither did I hesitate to confront a person in the moment of a needed correction. I tackled them sympathetically, compassionately and positively. No one complained.

Energy suffused my entire being, expanding my capabilities to an extraordinary extent. I was ready for any challenge. A kindly and compassionate confidence impelled me forward as never before. A benign joyfulness infused both body and soul throughout all my waking hours. This was so unlike my experience of the manic energising episodes at which I had previously marvelled. It also differed from the benign and blissful outcome of the months of meditative reading of Monsignor Buckley's book and the involuntary recitation of the mantra 'Jesus loves me'. The difference was subtle. This time I felt that I, in my very essential self, had been released from the past.

Just as the acupuncture had frequently stimulated explosions of invisible streams of fireworks from my fingers and toes, now, and in contrast, immense surges of energy pulsed painlessly outwards from my upper chest. This was so unexpected, and such a startling phenomenon in itself, that I didn't know what to think. It was beyond my control. It was a pleasant sensation, just as if vast amounts of pent-up energy were being discharged outwards in release through my rib cage and skin. I couldn't and still can't explain it. When I told one or two people about it, they looked at me and didn't comment.

Later, I recalled my acupuncturist's words while speaking to me shortly before the depression lifted. 'I've permitted the "shen" to move to your heart via the liver. Now your spirit is free to move about in your heart.' He was extremely pleased when I described these energy discharges to him. Before that, he had explained how depression prevented the normal movement of the spirit within the heart. He concluded, 'Some day you will experience this and you will know it.' I most certainly did when it occurred. The Chinese medical metaphors were so apt.

Another day, when I had been excitedly telling him all that was happening to me, he held up his hand. 'Be careful, my friend,' he cautioned. He paused, holding my gaze with a stern expression. 'You are experiencing a level of joy that you will never experience again in this life.'

He was correct. Twenty years and more on, nothing remotely like it has occurred since. It was an incredible privilege and a fascinating insight into the workings of body and mind. I accept that it won't happen again, in this world at least!

Throughout this entire joyous spell, I was totally in command of my faculties, except that my soft-spoken voice resonated with my inner confidence. My observing self could hear it. My once exaggerated cautiousness disappeared. Assertion became a normal response, whenever situations demanded. I could see the expressions of surprise in the features of my senior colleagues whenever I acted swiftly on some challenging issue. They knew that I had been cured, but they didn't enquire directly of me about it. Their queries reached me by word of mouth of others.

Contrary to what I describe, I later sensed that maybe it was my slowly ebbing paranoia that restrained me from speaking openly about my marvellous experiences. I didn't attempt to explain these occurrences to my wife. She had more than enough with which to grapple. There was so much going on in my life during that six-week period. She unfortunately perceived this to be yet another shift in my personality. It was understandable. Unwittingly, I was making life even more confusing for her. My compliant depressed nature had been nudged firmly aside. A confident, assured and outspoken husband, filled with energy and can-do, replaced the silent, sometimes compliant, and often withdrawn person she had known for so long. Sadly she never participated in that joyful inner euphoria that had lifted me from my dismal and distressed existence. It remained a private experience. In total contrast to my experiences, she became apprehensive and bewildered.

This wonderful episode lasted six weeks. Then the magnificent firmament of this heaven-sent release collapsed inwards and was gone. Bereft, I was my old, sad, if somewhat wiser, self.

XX

Following on my cure, and some time after the huge excitement of the euphoric episode of release had subsided, I experienced a series of panic attacks. I awoke from sleep one night frozen to my bed by an acute state of fear. It was frightening in the extreme. I was literally paralysed by a level of fear that hurt physically. It attached to nothing — there was no related cause. It presented itself as white fear, conjuring up in my mind the image of an immense iceberg. I sat up in bed, both hands spread firmly on the mattress. So intense was the sensation of terror that I couldn't endure another moment of it.

I woke my wife and attempted to explain what was happening to me. 'I'll have to phone Gerry,' I said.

'You can't phone him at three o'clock in the morning. He'll think you're mad.'

'But I can't take another moment of this,' I protested. 'You've no idea what it's like. I just can't. You don't understand.'

'You can't phone the man at this hour,' my wife insisted.

We argued back and forth. Finally I agreed, most reluctantly, to defer calling him until 7.30. I continued to sit upright on the bed, stricken by the worst fear I had ever experienced. I thought that the waiting would never end. Those dark morning hours in the company of the silent and fear-filled iceberg seemed an eternity.

When I called my acupuncturist, he listened carefully. 'Right, no problem, come over right away,' he said. 'That's no problem whatsoever. I'll be waiting. Get in your car and come right over.' His voice was calm.

'Don't you worry; we'll deal with this,' he reassured me when I entered his cottage clinic.

He proceeded to apply the needles as soon as I lay on his couch. I distinctly recall the needles that he inserted between my scalp and my skull. Other needles penetrated my upper lip with a crunching sound. There were others but I don't remember their locations.

In quite a short time, the fear began to subside. Gerry stood beside me, soothing and distracting me with reassuring words while I recovered. Finally he sent me on my way free of all terror, and I returned straight away to work. There were other but lesser panic attacks and Gerry continued the treatment until he was satisfied that the episodes were gone.

They didn't return, but an element of their trauma hung on for some time. I became uncharacteristically nervous about air travel. It wasn't so much the flying itself, but rather the prospect of finding myself separated by long distances from home and my acupuncturist. Fortunately, in time, all traces of the event passed away.

In the aftermath, I attempted to unravel the possible causes. Why, after an interval of weeks or months, did the panic attacks ever happen? I can only vaguely relate them to an incident that took place at night, on some undated occasion either preceding my recovery, or very soon after.

I awoke in the darkness to the absolute certainty of an evil presence — as I typed these words, the hairs on my neck stood on end at the recall of the incident. I was paralysed by fear of an evil presence in the bedroom. I believed that Satan was standing at the foot of the bed. His presence verged on the palpable. So fearful was I in the bed on that night that I couldn't move. Eventually, recalling a reference to the effectiveness of the Sign of the Cross, I ever so slowly willed my hand out from under the bedclothes and managed to bless myself. The menacing presence disappeared instantly.

XXI

Facing up to normal depression-free life was difficult. Losing the superior capabilities of that happy interlude, I had to come to terms with reality. In their absence, my life became ordinary and familiar. I was my old self, complete with all my inadequacies and insecurities. This new depression-free existence was inevitably peppered with challenges. I had to work through them, drawing on my experience. It wasn't that I was ungrateful. Rather, it was the significance of the adjustments that took time to encompass.

The mood swings of the past had been disturbing. I had zoomed from the very edge of a dark chasm upwards on to brilliantly sunny and joyous heights. As an insightful professional reader remarked on an early draft of my story, 'You've been to the moon and back.' His metaphor expressed it all. Now that I was cured, I was at the same time grounded. I repeatedly reminded myself that my will was freed of its previous, cloyingly fearful constraints. I reacted positively and confidently, as best I could, as needs arose.

All the excitement and bewilderment of those extraordinary changes passed on, and life receded to normality. I coped with life by using the resources that God has given me.

However, after many years, the very worst happened to me. Depression returned. I was shocked, horrified, terrified and dumbfounded. The coincidence of three unsought and stressful demands on my time and abilities stretched me a long way outside my comfort zone. Matters eventually got to me. It was most inopportune, not to mention being ominously disturbing. Certain familiar symptoms manifested themselves.

This time, I recognised the symptoms early on and ran to my GP. Antidepressants were prescribed. I considered travelling abroad in order to track down Gerry Longfield, my acupuncturist of the past. But there were arguments against this. He had ceased practising many years before, and he lived in a country where a licence was necessary before the skin of a patient could be broken.

In my diary, there was the name of a Chinese acupuncturist, penned in by myself. I have no recollection of who gave it to me. After some hesitation, I dialled the number. 'I'm sorry; he has retired,' an accented voice replied. My heart sank. I knew in my heart and soul that acupuncture was the only route to a cure. 'But Dr Lee would see you,' the voice suggested. For some reason, I was hesitant: I didn't know this person. But eventually I committed myself.

Dr Lee proved to be a young man with a developing command of English. At his first treatment, he didn't twist the needles. At the next encounter, there was still no twisting. At the third encounter, a Chinese translator was present. Our communication was easier. She was an impressive and highly intelligent person who stood a little to one side of the acupuncturist. 'You're not twisting the needles,' I remarked.

Instantly their features were wreathed in smiles. 'Our clients don't like it. It hurts,' Dr Lee explained. We laughed. I was so relieved.

'I want to be hurt,' I asserted.

While my treatment progressed, my GP referred me to a senior psychologist in a public hospital. I was so impressed by her questioning that I asked her if she would take me on as a patient. 'I'm sorry, but I'm not permitted,' she said, smiling. She referred me to two other psychiatrists. I told them all I was attending an acupuncturist. I also told Dr Lee about my medications. None expressed concerns.

As the weeks passed, I observed my symptoms carefully, and eventually I concluded that this unwanted depression was a mild version. There was no pain. Neither did the demons arrive. My willpower was not greatly affected. I responded to needs immediately and without significant difficulty.

Dr Lee assured me that I would be cured, and so I was. My relief was immense, though I was slow to believe that the depression had gone. 'I can feel it in your pulse and see it in your tongue, in your face and in your eyes,' said this warm-hearted acupuncturist, whom I had learned to trust. 'Yes, you are better. You need to come once more.' As a precaution, I arranged to attend Dr Lee every quarter. It was a comforting and reassuring arrangement.

In retrospect, it was all so quick that I haven't adjusted even as I write. It was a salutary experience, though, and I can't help thinking that I was insufficiently grateful for my first cure. Possibly God was sending a warning, I reflected. My psychiatrist explained that I would be prone to relapses once I had been depressed. It is a feature of the illness. The fact that she lives locally is most reassuring. She amended my medication slightly and my doubts about my recovery disappeared.

* * *

This concludes the story of my illness. The first part of this book has revealed the inner realities of depression, as experienced by me. It also records the means by which I coped. I hope that these may provide positive insights for those suffering from depression, as well for those living in close contact with the depressed. The following chapters elaborate on my experiences of acupuncture and reflexology, which together cured my depression. They also explore in greater detail the crucial aspects of my experiences. These may prove to be of interest to those currently suffering from depression and also their families, close friends and colleagues.

I should mention the importance of empathising with the sufferer where possible. For those in the minding or caring role, I suggest that they read up and enquire their way into the mind and the world of the depressed. I appreciate that this is a genuine challenge but if it is taken up, the minder will be better equipped to empathise with the depressed. An awareness of where the depressed is and how and to what extent he or she is suffering would create a level of mutual understanding that could ease life for both parties.

Part Two

ON REFLECTION

Acupuncture and Reflexology

This is a brief commentary of my encounter with acupuncture, a practice that first surfaced in China as long ago as 4,000 years. Its very age mesmerises. How on earth did those ancient Chinese medical practitioners ever happen upon this treatment? Of course, we shouldn't be surprised. They were equipped with exactly the same intelligence as contemporary man who is forging extraordinary discoveries.

The earliest needles were fashioned from stone. Just imagine the painstaking effort required to chip and chip at a fragment of appropriate stone in order to fashion something crudely resembling the sharpness of a needle. A sharp point would have been the basic requisite. There are, of course, rocks like flint that lend themselves to being patiently fashioned to produce sharp edges and points, but I don't know how they managed for disinfectants.

To my mind, the big intellectual jump lay in their astonishing ability to discern the existence of Qi (or 'chee' as it is pronounced), an energy form. They further discovered that it streams along meridians or lines in the body. It was along these same meridians that they uncovered points that connected directly to particular body organs. Thousands of years passed in the evolution of this medicine. However, modern-day science has not uncovered the mysteries of Qi other than to discover that its speed of travel is somewhat slower than the speed of light.

The Qi flows along twelve major meridians that form a pattern of the major organ reference system. Along these meridians are 365 acupuncture points where needles are inserted depending on which organ is being treated.

Traditional Chinese medicine views the healthy body as being in a delicate state of balance between the opposing forces of yin and yang. Yin is the cold, slow, passive principle. Yang is the hot, excited and active principle. When the yin energy and the yang energy are out of balance, Qi becomes blocked, thereby giving rise to illnesses. Chinese medical practitioners believe that inserting needles at the blocked or impeded points releases the pent-up energy, thus restoring the normal balance of yin and yang, and eventually inducing a return to good health.

Illness suggests a pressure imbalance in the body system of energy. Electricity appeared to fit this notion but the identification of its slower speed discounts this. My personal experience of the shock created when a needle penetrated an appropriate point on a meridian suggested an electric shock. However, this wasn't correct. What I experienced was a discharge of the energy, Qi.

In China, acupuncture is used for pain relief, as in surgery for instance. It is, of course, also used widely in the treatment of other illnesses. By Western medical terms, it would be a surgical analgesia. Chinese surgeons claim that one-third of patients being operated on receive adequate analgesia via acupuncture alone. The same analgesia is believed, in China, to be superior to Western drug-based analgesics because normal bodily functions are maintained throughout an operation and acupuncture is non-intrusive. My experience certainly confirmed this. However, US surgeons have stated that acupuncture works as an analgesic for only ten per cent of patients.

Sadly, acupuncture doesn't work for every one. In this respect, I was truly fortunate. In my initial enthusiasm, I recommended it to a number of depressives. Hearing of my cure, they made contact with me or with my wife, and I was naively enthusiastic. A number of these enquirers had no reaction whatsoever to acupuncture, and I was embarrassed by their disappointments. Afterwards, I stood well back and thought deeply about helping fellow sufferers.

I believe that I was also fortunate in the acupuncturist recommended to me. We empathised. He was happy to answer my questions, and I never let up enquiring. My curiosity impelled me to find out as much as I could about a medicine that cured where Western medicine had failed me miserably. Its very strangeness stimulated my questioning. Frequently my acupuncturist would leave the room and return with a massive tome, from which he read in amplification of his explanations.

How acupuncture works remains a mystery. One of those ancient ancestral Chinese acupuncturists must have looked at the human body in exasperation, exclaiming, 'There just has to be a way' to cure this illness. Eventually, through the insight of a forgotten genius, a new cure was discovered, leading on over thousands of years to its present evolution.

The penetration of a needle through the skin at an appropriate point induces a painful release of energy just like an electrical discharge. The skin immediately surrounding the point becomes heated, and tiny beads of perspiration can become manifest. Twisting the needle increases the intensity of this reaction. That was how it felt while I was being treated. I grimaced and exclaimed at the bigger shocks. Frequently these shocks were accompanied by a curious sensation, as if invisible sparks were racing outwards from the tips of either my fingers or my toes.

Generally, in the instance of my first acupuncturist, these points were located on and about the base of my right-hand thumb. These and several other points on my limbs were needled, including a number on my right leg and foot. On completion of this process, I was left to rest on the couch for approximately twenty minutes. I relaxed into a most pleasant state of restful and warming ease. When the time was up, the acupuncturist extracted the needles carefully, pressing the tiny wound with a sterilised pad to halt any bleeding.

Somehow the bursts of energy I experienced stimulated unknown curatives within my body, which, with progressive twice-weekly treatments, led to my healing. The treatment sessions spanned ten weeks.

Reflexology is based on the discovery that particular areas of the soles of the feet are connected to the major organs. Reflexologists massage the soles of their patients' feet enabling them to assess a patient's state of health. Malfunctioning organs are signalled by the painful sensitivity of the related areas of the soles. This process itself can be a curative. I experienced a dramatic instance of this when, some months following my cure, I suffered terrifying panic attacks. My acupuncturist was suddenly taken ill while he was treating me for these attacks. I was alarmed to find him departing his clinic by ambulance as I arrived for a session. His son, a reflexologist, received me in the clinic. 'Look, I'll do some reflexology on you. It'll help. I know it will,' he said, smiling encouragingly.

As he vigorously massaged my feet, his hands felt like steel. Having recovered from the depression, I had fewer sensitive areas, and I began to relax as he worked over my feet. Following a prolonged session, the sense of panic had all but disappeared. I was immensely relieved and went immediately to work.

Fortunately my acupuncturist returned a week later. The

panic attacks subsided under his acupuncture and eventually disappeared permanently. It was an insightful experience, which demonstrated the complementary nature of the two treatments.

Symptoms, SAD and Related Matters

S triving to describe my depression and its effects proved stubbornly challenging. So much so that on several occasions I considered abandoning this book. However, an inner voice urged me on. It reminded me that I had always been reluctant to give up on a task or challenge, once committed to it. It was a facet of my nature.

Depression is a mood state wherein the spirit is so downcast that the body is affected. It is as if it is drawn downwards in sympathy. Everything looks bleakly grey. 'Darkness' is the word constantly evoked when my mind shifts to thinking about depression. Pessimism pervades.

The word depression, to me, is expressive of a kind of lifelessness. The moods of a depressive are bowed down under the sheer weight of the sombre illness that is clamped on the mind. The highs and lows of normal life are levelled out. When a happy occasion arises in a healthy being, life is good, often joyful and well worth living. Such respites from the ordinariness of life give it colour. Depression, in contrast, dampens down joy, all but excluding it. Existence survives in a grey, downbeat fog.

Taking action on any task, even the very smallest, demands abnormal efforts of will. Depression clamps a restraining inertia on the sufferer's will, against which he or she struggles incessantly, year in and year out. Living from day to day becomes an unrelenting and steeply uphill struggle in which sufferers must force themselves into action at all times.

Depression undermines self-confidence. It fastens on the slightest suggestion of confidence and delivers negative asides instead, dressing them up into compelling arguments.

Pain

The level of accompanying pain, the pain of depression, is a permanent and disturbing intrusion on the depressive's everyday life. It is a strange, frightening and all-enveloping pain, and one that differs from normal everyday pains. A fall, a bump, a cramp, a cut, the dentist's drilling or a wrenched muscle are commonplace sources of pain. An upset stomach or flu brings its particular pains. Depression is vastly different, though. It brings with it a most unwelcome and all-enveloping suffering that defies description. It alters the entire life of its sufferer.

One day, two years or more after I had been cured of depression, I was working at my desk when a sharp and surging pain occurred in the centre of my chest. I tried to shrug it off, thinking that it was an inconsequential spasm, but its increasing intensity was such that I became frightened and began to perspire. I was convinced that it was a heart attack, and went into shock. Fortunately someone entered my office at that moment and, realising that I was seriously ill, called an ambulance. In a matter of minutes, I was brought to the Accident and Emergency department of a nearby hospital.

The staff in the A & E room wired me up to a monitor and discovered no signs of a heart attack, but meanwhile the pain continued to intensify to the point where I became nauseated. I wanted to be sick, but I couldn't. The doctors were undecided as to the cause of the pain and I was admitted to a public ward, where I lay, writhing in pain behind my bed curtains. Painkillers brought temporary relief but I spent a most uncomfortable night.

The following day, I was moved to a private room, where a doctor informed me that I was suffering from a kidney stone. My relief was immense but the pain endured. I eventually found a measure of comfort, simply by gripping my arms tightly about my midriff while walking around in tight circles. I could appreciate the humour in the appearance presented to visitors. During those hours of circling between bed and walls and freed of the worst of my discomfort, it dawned on me that this pain was by no means the worst I had experienced. It was quite unlike the pain of depression.

First of all, this pain was transient. It had a beginning and would cease as soon as the stone that was obstructing my kidney duct was removed. It was a finite, physical pain, attached to a particular organ, and it differed from the all-pervading and all-consuming pain of depression. Furthermore, it didn't remotely impinge on my soul. Whereas depression bound both body and soul together in its grip and its appalling pain, this particular physical pain was entirely different. The difference between the pain that I was enduring and the pain of depression lay in the lack of a spiritual element in the former. I was elated at this discovery. At that instant, I realised that the pain of depression had been affecting my entire being, both my physical body and my soul.

My eminent psychiatrist's words echoed in my mind from the past: 'The core pain of melancholia is the worst suffering known to man.' Now it dawned on me, in the hospital room, that my soul had been in pain for almost thirty years. It was also absolutely clear to me that this kidney-stone pain, appalling though it was, was a far lesser and a vastly more tolerable form of suffering. 'Great,' I exclaimed to myself!

I realised also that I could think with absolute clarity despite the intense pain that the pebble in my kidney duct was generating. I even regained my sense of humour. I couldn't wait to see the offending stone. When it eventually clanged into the stainless-steel jug, the pain eased and dispersed in a short time.

Sadness

A depressive sighs for the loss of his or her good health and all its associated freedoms: the loss of the ability to relate easily to others; the loss of the ability to relax; the loss of joyful moments; the loss of certain social skills; and on and on to the loss of virtually all that is good in life. It seems to me that the depressive experiences sadness to a remarkable extent, but the sadness that attaches to depression is often entirely obscured by the more intrusive symptoms of the illness.

It is a melancholy illness, strangely sad and beyond mere words. Joy is all but excluded from the heart of the sufferer. The symptoms of the depression can be of such severity that they obliterate any consciousness of any underlying sadness. The pain of my depression alone, I feel, would have masked any gentle sadness.

Occasionally I observed my American brother heaving deep sighs while I was on holidays with him. I associated these with his prevailing sadness at the complex and unending difficulties he was experiencing in his marriage. I suspected also that he might have been depressed, and I raised the possibility with him once. He brushed it off. 'Everybody gets depressed,' he muttered dismissively. I didn't pursue the matter.

I didn't know until after his death that my brother had a serious heart problem, and this alone must have blighted his life. On reflection, I believe that he was in denial about this condition. In any case, he had many reasons for his sadness.

From earliest childhood we had been close. We were more than just brothers. I missed him deeply in his going.

Fear

Fear dominated my life under depression. It arrived at the very outset, on the day when I hooked the sea bass. Thereafter it was present throughout my waking hours. It proved to be extremely unsettling company and entirely altered my interior world. It was, of course, a symptom of the illness. Regrettably I'm not equipped to analyse it in any depth, other than to record its occurrence.

Once, when speaking to a group that included a therapist, I mentioned a practice that I devised to deal with the fears that caused anxious and relentless turmoil during my waking hours, long before dawn. Uncontrollable, these fears imagined the very worst outcomes to the challenges confronting me in the day ahead, as they streamed across my conscious mind. Fortunately, at some point, I realised that the following day's events rarely turned out as bad as visualised while lying in bed. Reflecting on this, I began to imagine situations far worse than those I had ever apprehended. This was done in a spirit of curiosity. I wanted to see if it was possible to fool myself sufficiently to make the oncoming day less stressful and less painful. Remarkably it worked. The oncoming day proved invariably to be easier. I persisted with this practice up until my depression lifted. Innocently, in my own way, I was facing down my fears.

When I finished relating this, the therapist in the audience enquired if I had discovered this by my own efforts.

'Yes,' I replied.

'Well, that's a recognised therapy. Didn't you know that? It's bringing oneself to face one's fears,' she elaborated.

Vivification of Experience

I became accustomed to this happy phenomenon, described in the first part of this book, but I never took it for granted. On recovery, this intriguing enhancement of pleasures vanished. One day, I noticed it was gone. I missed it deeply. Now, writing about it eighteen years on, that enhancement has been securely replaced by normal levels of enjoyment.

Seasonal Affective Disorder (SAD)

In the first autumn following my cure, I sensed the onset of an ailment not altogether unlike depression, but it certainly wasn't the depression that I had known for so long. Even though it was painless, I was deeply disturbed. I had had more than enough of the illness. Reasoning with myself, I appreciated that it was different and that it was a more benign mood shift, and vastly less unpleasant than depression. While my mood was certainly down, it was in no way accompanied by physical suffering of any kind. It was a worry but not a serious one.

As it happened, very soon afterwards, I read an article about Seasonal Affective Disorder. I was immensely relieved. Serendipity, no less, brought me in contact with a man whom I had known years previously in a work-related context. He was by then marketing light-boxes, among other items. He went on to introduce me to people in England who were promoting an awareness of SAD and its implications. Some of them visited Cork, on a promotional trip. They were marvellously positive people and full of good cheer. I enviously marvelled at their enthusiasm and upbeat attitudes.

The acquisition of a light-box introduced me to full-spectrum lighting and its beneficial effects. Very simply, full-spectrum light can be used to extend the hours of daylight and thus ward off SAD. The light is visibly close to the character of sunlight, though, of course, less intense. A maximum of four hours per day while reading or relaxing in front of a light-box cleared up my SAD in a matter of three weeks or so. Eventually I experienced autumns free of the malaise. Nowadays I place a light-box on the breakfast and evening meal table, when I sense the slightest onset of SAD. In a matter of days, any recurring symptoms disappear. It's magical.

Alcohol and Depression

Alcohol is a depressant. Furthermore, on the few occasions when I ever became mildly drunk, I found the experience of a hangover to be so awful that it became a useful deterrent. I developed a dislike of the sensation of losing full control of my wits, even while mildly inebriated. Thereafter I developed respect for the downside of drinking alcohol.

I also learned that stress and alcohol did not mix, at least as far as my body concerned. Neither, of course, did depression and alcohol mix. This mixture delivered a most appalling hangover. I was extremely fortunate that drinking never became a prop. Today, a glass of wine before my evening meal is a pleasant punctuation to my day.

Developing Strategies for Coping

I didn't have a plan for coping with my illness. I could never have anticipated the trials and nature of the situations that were to come. As those events occurred, I reacted to them and dealt with them as best I could. Frequently I was either confounded or fearfully bewildered. Months often passed before a new coping stratagem suggested itself. Nevertheless, my coping techniques evolved.

The impediments of the illness taxed my innermost resources to their absolute limits. Had I been well during the years of illness, there would have been more than enough to occupy my mind. As it was, it was a wonder that I got anything done. Between a growing family and work, there were endless demands on my time. Helping to raise a large family and at the same time managing an onerous professional business, the pressures were unrelenting. Apart from these, I was greatly distracted by the array of symptoms, and also the unpleasant side-effects of certain medications. This meant that I was acting, deciding, knowing, reacting, reasoning, discriminating and thinking under formidable handicaps. However, I did manage to function usefully throughout my working years.

Interacting with others usefully dispersed the symptoms of the illness, if only temporarily. Absorbing elements of my work, like design tasks, attending meetings, or dictating letters or long reports, freed me temporarily from the worst effects of the illness. One way or another, it was an endless learning and striving process. When my mind was fully occupied, it would transcend the very worst of the symptoms. It might take an hour or so of continuous mental effort before I could achieve this relatively balanced state. Once there, though, life was tolerable. This occurred both in personal interactions with others and while I was absorbed in a compelling task. Sadly this transcending of the symptoms was no more than a series of intermittent reliefs, but it certainly helped me to perform as situations demanded.

My real difficulties occurred when work ceased at the end of the day. Normal relaxation was impossible and I immediately became vulnerable. The pain returned in its greatest intensity. Furthermore, the demons of depression returned *en masse*, taking over my inner unseen life and submerging me in a black, tortured gloom. When this happened, I struggled to seek positive, affirming and occupying distractions. My wife's company was one such, but it wasn't always possible for her to give me her undivided attention. For her, I had become an uncomfortable, downbeat and over-demanding presence. This relentless need of her attention sometimes led to arguments and misunderstandings.

In the first part of the book, I discussed the marvellous release that running conferred on me. This exercising was a vital feature of my coping. But for it, I doubt that I would have survived. Acting initially on intuition, I ran for all of thirty years. The release of painkilling endorphins into my brain enabled me to persist in my struggles.

Reading rarely failed to provide a release. It was a stabilising recreation. I read widely and it was possible, most times, to lose myself in a good book. However, I needed silence, and this created its own difficulties and conflicts. Our six children had an ingenious capacity for being noisy.

The cinema, better-quality films particularly, also lifted the worst of the symptoms. However, as I walked out of the cinema and into the streets, the depression instantly slammed down on me, dispersing the cinematic dream state that I had been enjoying.

Tiredness contributed its negative burdens. It made evenings hellish, and the consequent gloom affected my wife. No effort of will on my part could disperse those black moods. Time and time again, television was a saviour: a most welcome distraction. There were family-oriented programmes that we all watched and enjoyed. Other times, my wife and I enjoyed our favourite programmes.

In an effort to cope with my illness, I gradually devised a range of strategies. I realised that our attitudes are vital influences in our life. They can make such a difference. Reading Norman Vincent Peale's *The Power of Positive Thinking* opened my mind to my earliest strivings against depression. This book held my attention in the early years of my illness. Repeated readings of that once very popular book helped me to think just a shade more positively. It suggested a realistic choice: giving in to negative thoughts or seeking the positive options. It was one thing to be aware of the latter but trying to push aside the depression-driven negativity was another. In time, I exhausted the contents of that compact book, yet something of its inherent philosophy adhered permanently on my mind.

Later on, I began reading two pages of the New Testament every evening in bed. Reading them with all the concentration I could muster, I recorded many striking inspirational quotations, entering them in a notebook. I pursued this spiritual reading throughout the latter of the worst years. It was a fail-safe resource. Without it, I might not have survived. What I read provided a measure of inner strength, mental stability, reassurance and an infusion of hope. Putting it another way, this reading nurtured my hopes for some future time when matters might improve. Although I was unaware of it at the time, it most likely reinforced what little faith I had.

These spiritual readings also stilled my inner tortures to a considerable extent, while I sat in bed, propped up by pillows. No matter how many times I read passages of the New Testament, each new reading delivered fresh and reassuring insights.

Later again, two of Norman Peale's books brought more strength and comfort. They even stilled something of the worst of later panic attacks that followed on my cure. *The Treasury of Courage and Confidence* and *The Treasury of Joy and Enthusiasm* travelled everywhere with me. These are remarkable compilations, their contents drawn from many sources, including sacred and medical. They delivered inspiration and reassurance when I desperately needed it. They quietened my worst agitations. Gratefully, today I don't need them.

Peale's books record extracts of the writings of numerous inspirational authors of all creeds. Their content didn't defeat the pessimism of the depression, but the books provided an inner core of stabilising strength when crises assailed me. They steadied my inner resources, enlarging the positive resources of my mind, thus helping me to fight off the negative demons that relentlessly nagged day and night.

During a further and darker phase of depression, it dawned on me that, possibly, I wasn't doing enough to help. I noticed that whenever my mind freewheeled into daydreaming, it invariably fed in many negative thoughts and resentments. These, of course, made me extremely vulnerable. Driving unaccompanied on long journeys was a typical and particularly vulnerable situation. My mind invariably drifted. There was insufficient occupation to hold my mind's attention. Far too often, I drove on automatic pilot.

As mentioned earlier, running was a crucial method of self-help. However, solitary exercising often led my mind into random downbeat reveries. Keeping my mind positively and usefully focused proved difficult. To combat these situations, I brought cards with me on which I had recorded extracts from my inspirational note-taking. At the commencement of car journeys, I used to fix one or two to the dash in my car. I also kept some of the cards in a jacket pocket at all times, while I sealed others to waterproof them against rain while running. Thus equipped, I had positive reading material to hand wherever I happened to be: driving, running, sitting in a train or on a plane. This practice injected positivisms onto my mind, and was unfailingly reassuring.

Talking about my illness had the effect of actually increasing its overwhelming and unrelenting presence. At the same time, this upset those listening to me, who were aware of my condition. In the earliest years of the depression, there were occasions when the need to unburden myself overwhelmed me. It rapidly became apparent that those close to me most definitely didn't want to listen to my downbeat ramblings on my unseen illness. Some became more than forcefully vocal. One, in response to my unburdening myself, regaled me with an extended list of my shortcomings. Shocked at this entirely unexpected outburst, I determined never again to mention my illness to anyone. This, in turn, prompted me to be ever on my guard to act as normally as possible at all times, no matter how low I felt. Besides, I reminded myself that if I didn't want people in general to know about my condition, logically I shouldn't mention it myself.

Fortunately in my youth I had developed something of an ability to endure. Years of unhappy schooling and excessive punishment had given me many opportunities to practise enduring. I had also endured bullying in my earlier years at school. These trials provided useful training in the endurance of unpleasant circumstances. I learned to put up with abuse and carry on.

Climbing afforded experiences comparable to those of cycling, as discussed in the first part of this book. Hill walking is the term used today. On certain days, mountain inclines could be challenging in the extreme. Maybe I was tired before I set out. Perhaps there had been a lapse in my training. On a mountain, it was essential to stay with the group; it could even be a matter of survival. I just hung on and hung on when things were going badly for me.

My love of mountains and climbing endured well beyond middle age, indeed, and into my senior years. It had begun in childhood. When my father would point out the peaks of the west Cork and Kerry mountains, I would scrutinise them intently, wondering what it would be like to clamber up their slopes. My mother's home in Dublin had an impressive tall stair-window that gave a view to the gently curving summits of the Dublin and Wicklow mountains. The marginal panes were coloured. By moving my head laterally I could change the colours of these mystical slopes. The story of Red Hugh O'Donnell's escape from Dublin Castle and his flight to the same mountains held my boyhood imagination. These were some of the stimuli that led on to a passionate attachment.

Underlying the physical nature of climbing was the persistent conviction that God was somehow closer to me whenever I arrived breathless and panting on a summit. Time and time again, following hours on toilsome and steep slopes, I sensed a presence that I judged could only be God. While resting with my companions and looking down upon the world around us, I often experienced a sense of peaceful fulfilment. Climbing friends confirm similar experiences. The accompanying solitude of mountains was another deep-seated attraction. This sense of separation from the everyday world and its demands and pressures created a similar sense of security to that of an inaccessible refuge. It provided a welcome and silent respite for reflection and mental clarification.

In my late sixties I participated in treks in the Himalayas and the Andes. I wouldn't have missed these experiences for anything.

Coping is about persisting with the challenges of life and never giving up. Participating in each of my recreations demanded physical suffering that was often intense. Too often, it was hugely tempting – especially when cycling in the past when leg muscles screamed with pain – to throw in the towel and lie down to rest on the road's verge. At those times, I vowed that I would never again participate, such was the intensity of the suffering. No matter what the exhaustion or muscular stiffness in the aftermath of an event, though, in a matter of a day or two I was once more impatient to participate in the next race. Mountain expeditions provided parallel experiences. There were times when, approaching a summit in a storm of horizontal rain, I vowed that I would never again forsake the warmth and comfort of home. Yet, within a day or two, I would be planning the next outing.

This stubborn streak – maybe it was obstinacy – was to become my rearguard in coping. Whenever matters were about to overwhelm me, my inherent and obstinate nature would goad me on to endure.

Facing the day was invariably daunting. There was no escaping the early-morning prospect of apparently insuperable tasks and challenges. At some time, close to my impending cure, I devised a mental process that helped. Early in my commuter journey to work I would mentally review the immediate tasks and challenges ahead, and resolve to overcome them. This usually took place as I was rounding a scenic bend on the tidal estuary not far from my home. Trees overhung the waters. On still mornings, they were reflected on the surface. In time, I christened this corner 'Resolution Bend'.

In some long-forgotten reading, I learned that praying for others could be an antidote for despair. It's a form of giving or of acting unselfishly. If I prayed for others, God would hear those prayers as well as those I had offered for my own cure. I explored this practice. If nothing else, it would usefully occupy my mind. Practising unselfishness had to be beneficial, I reasoned. To my mind, it's a private form of giving. 'It is in giving that we receive.' I tried it and it certainly worked for me.

I eventually used to practise this on car journeys, which were a feature of my professional work. It was necessary to supervise site works on a regular basis and to chair the site meetings. While I enjoyed driving, in practical terms this practice of praying broke up the inevitable tedium of long hours at the wheel. On lengthy journeys, I first recited the rosary. Then I prayed for a long list of deceased relatives and friends. I prayed for those who were ill. I prayed for the living and the dead, including those since gone. I memorised this list as it grew. This surprised me, as I had never been proficient at memorising.

Despite the mental effort involved, this practice added a new purpose to journeys. More importantly, it kept my mind focused on positive matters. It reduced, to a large extent, the distracting and disturbing intrusions of the discursive mind. It furthermore countered the self-absorption that is a feature of depression, and which can lead on to selfishness and self-pity.

Once, during an extremely painful passage of depression, and at the end of a working day in Dublin, I collapsed into the seat of the evening train. It had been a long, demanding and tiring ten hours of meetings. Fatigued and encumbered by pain, I hugely appreciated the prospect of three hours of isolation.

The train had by then become a predictable but transient refuge. No one could get at me other than fellow passengers. It was in the era prior to the advent of mobile phones.

Anyway, unable to shake off the pain of depression on that particular afternoon, something — I don't know what — prompted me to relax entirely into the very worst of the pain and depression, and experience its darkest depths. I did precisely that. I closed my eyes and let my entire being slide into the very depths of the pain. To my surprise, the pain eased remarkably, and I became relatively comfortable and relaxed. I was startled, amazed and pleased. I sat there, silent and inactive, wondering at the mental and biochemical mechanisms that brought about this unexpected easing of my sufferings. I probably congratulated myself prematurely on discovering this new painkiller. I can't recall how long the pain remained eased, but at the time I was excitedly impressed.

Naturally I sought to repeat the exercise. The mental effort involved was enormous. Only a slight measure of relief was experienced; it was nothing like that of the first instance. I attempted the exercise repeatedly, but the significant effort entailed defeated me. It wasn't possible to re-attain that initial and marvellous relief.

It is possible that on that first instance, I wasn't anticipating anything in the way of a positive outcome: I merely relaxed as best I could and did nothing else. However, the next time I was probably straining for a positive result and consequently not relaxing into total inactivity. In doing so, I possibly defeated, in part at least, the relaxing process, and sadly the anticipated effect did not manifest itself. I was seeking a result.

Faith

From an early age, I had searched for the meaning of life. I yearned to explore, study and understand its still inexplicable regions. I wished to get my mind entirely around it. I didn't know then the reply Albert Einstein had once given when asked about the meaning of human life: 'To find a satisfactory answer to this question it is essential to be religious.' How encouraging this insight would have been for me in those disturbed times! In any event, I failed to apply myself to a constructive investigation of the true meaning of life. I had too many compelling obligations and responsibilities.

My attachment to religion surely stemmed from my parents' fervent and exemplary practice of their Roman Catholic faith. Probably it was reinforced by the elements of religious knowledge absorbed from the Christian Brothers at school. It was one of the few subjects that consistently held my attention.

Much later, during the years of illness, and when, daily, I was reading two pages of the New Testament, I noticed Jesus' insistent emphasis on the value of faith and the need to acquire it. Up to that point, I had never really contemplated faith. I was, however, impressed by His insistent reminders in some of the spiritual quotations that I liked. Gradually they adhered in my consciousness. My thinking on the subject had been muddled up to then. Of course, Monsignor Buckley's sharp comment helped.

The words 'Faith, Hope and Charity' have an old-fashioned ring to them today. Nevertheless, despite my tendency to inattention, the words somehow stamped themselves indelibly on my mind. It was a pity that I didn't engage with them and research their meanings and intent at a much earlier age. I mention them as evidence that I did, at least, hope for a cure throughout all the years of depression. Missing out on the reality of faith didn't help me, yet I believe that the depth of my yearning for a cure contained an element of belief in itself. I absolutely believed that God would cure me, if He so willed.

Verse eleven of Paul's Letter to the Hebrews commences as follows: 'Now faith is an assurance of things hoped for, a conviction of things not seen; for because of it the men of old had divine testimony borne to them.' I uncovered this stunning definition through prolonged researches. Then, in attempting to get my mind around this insight, or possibly adapting from another and now forgotten source, I somehow ended up with a simplified version: 'Faith is being sure of what we hope for and certain of what we do not see.' Possibly it is even a matter of self-belief. The impact of these quotations on my questing mind was immense. After all previous searches and strivings, I finally had a firm handle on the meaning of the word 'faith'. My years of lazy intellectual confusion vanished. It was immensely encouraging.

Then it occurred to me that a gift of positive thinking might well be related to faith. Positive thinking is arguably a matter of believing in possibilities when prevailing events might indicate negativity. It's being assured of possibilities, even while the precise outcome of the same possibilities cannot be foreseen with certainty. From that time on, I prayed for the gift of faith. 'I believe, Lord; please help my unbelief,' became my prayer thereafter.

At some time following my cure, it seemed that if I had been gifted with a deep and abiding faith, I might not have become depressed. It was an enticing idea, and one that seemed to be confirmed by a number of incidents. Sadly I was distracted from a preoccupation with faith. Those persistent doubts, insecurities, anxieties and fears that had dogged my life prior to the arrival of depression surely wouldn't have been able to slip under the guardian gates of faith, or so I theorised. However, once I recognised my genetic predisposition to depression, my ideas about this concept collapsed.

As I began making efforts at helping myself in coping with the depression, I also endeavoured to adopt a much more positive outlook on life. I wasn't very successful, but I believed that by focusing on the positive, I was helping myself. I had noticed enviously how positive people invariably faced life with remarkable assurance and confidence. Today, I know a man who unfailingly exudes the most positive of attitudes. Even his voice resonates with the vibrations of this extraordinary self-confidence, or maybe it is self-assurance. He is so positive in his attitudes that my mind sometime tires while listening to him. 'No one can be as positive as that,' my silent inner mind protests. Recently I observed him from a distance while he coped with a formidable reverse in his business affairs. His situation worried me greatly. The fact that he is married to one of my daughters concentrated my mind. He set about solving his difficulties with remarkable courage and confidence. Within an extraordinarily short period of time, he overcame the reverse and his business flourished. Was this an instance of faith, profoundly positive thinking, or was it self-belief? I'm not certain.

Even today, the mention of the word 'faith' invariably sends a gentle tremor coursing through my system. Faith, to my mind, is belief in the possibilities of life. Another way of putting it is the attainment of self-belief. 'If thou canst believe, all things are possible to him who believeth.' When the worst of my depression was grinding my inner self into particles, I used to repeat this quotation to myself while awaiting the onset of sleep. I did this with such determination that on waking one morning I was involuntarily babbling the very same words to myself.

Another find was 'Fear knocked on the door. Faith opened it. There was no one there.' I loved the implied drama of this quotation. There is a depth of conviction in it that lifts and inspires the sagging mind.

In my researches I was also, if unconsciously, looking for the means of transcending fear. Fear can and does promote despair and hopelessness. These, in turn, can engender such a convincing depth of worthlessness that suicide might well be prompted. An antidote is available in the words, 'Be bold and great forces will come to your aid.' They do come.

'With God nothing is impossible' was a frequent source of reassurance when I faced obstacles. Other quotations put it differently: 'The things that are impossible with men are possible with God.' 'I'm not afraid; with God all things are possible.'

Looking back, sometimes I wonder what prompted me to pursue Monsignor Buckley – which was uncharacteristic of me – and to persuade him to meet me. I am shy at the best of times. In turn, what prompted him and his friends to travel significant distances to meet me, a stranger, and spend an entire day praying over me? Why was I later gifted with that marvellous six weeks of blissful existence? Why did a friend, a journalist, suggest that I meet the intercessor? What prompted the shy lady to reveal her private past of depression and insist that I see the acupuncturist who had cured her? I can only believe that these and other related incidents and encounters were nothing less than manifestations of divine intervention.

When Monsignor Buckley told me that I had no faith, I was indignant. However, when I digested his remark, I truly appreciated his directness. He certainly made me think, and think deeply. Not alone did I think, but I began my two-year search for the meaning of the word 'faith'. My illness had undermined my level of self-belief, and whenever others challenged my views, I was only too ready to accept their opinions, believing that I was incorrect. I was neither being my true self, nor believing in myself.

Whatever Monsignor Buckley discerned in that single-page life account, his timing was brilliant. Even though he could not have known that at the time, he hit me hard at an extremely low point in my life. On reflection, his words prompted me to look coldly to myself, and to get on with doing something positive with my life and by my own efforts.

Suicide

Suicide is a link in the chronology of my story. In my three encounters with it, I was absolutely stunned by its ability to persuade me coolly to explore and consider my very own annihilation. The suicidal thoughts arrived without the slightest warning of their onset. In an instant, I was confronted, right in my face, as it were, with the enormous attractiveness of suicide in the context of the extremely negative phase of my life at the time. On three successive occasions, I was subjected to powerful and intensely seductive inner arguments to kill myself.

Words fail me in attempting to relate the progress of my thoughts throughout each of those incidents. Yes, I did wilfully desire to depart this life, but under the pressure of compelling and persuasive pressures.

At that time, I was coping with possibly the severest phase of my depression. Abruptly, from nowhere, I was further overcome by a sense of absolute worthlessness. I believed that I was of no use to anybody. I rejected myself entirely. At one moment, I had been grappling with a writing task, searching for appropriate words. The next instant, I was planning my demise. It was as abrupt as that. This intrusive notion exercised an extraordinary power over my thinking. I just couldn't get it out of my mind. It defeated the resources of both my rational mind and my already weakened willpower. Under its spell, I became totally irrational. I absolutely believed that I was of no value or use to those around me, most of all to my family. Rather, I believed that I was a burden on them, an unwanted and potentially destructive obstacle in their way. The sooner I took myself out of the way of my family, the better it would be for them. That was precisely my belief at the time.

While grappling with this pressured suggestion and, at the same time, carrying on with my normal life, I was aware that I was observing my very own being developing a strategy to end my life. I reviewed various ways of dying, from the point of view of which would be the swiftest and the least painful. I rejected drowning. I didn't like the notion of suffocating. A high-speed impact offered the best solution. I was convinced of the efficacy of this course. It was as simple as managing a car-borne high-speed impact against an immovable object.

Attachments to the material world are among the obstacles to attaining true contentment in life. We race about seeking happiness, excitement and gratification here, there and everywhere. We seek wealth in the belief that it will deliver happiness. The problem is, after each indulgence there follows a sadness and disappointment, a sense of being let down. The pleasure evaporates when we return to reality. What do we do? Ever hopeful, we return to the cycle again!

Suicidal unfortunates are also caught up in the same futile search to attain happiness. In their instance, life can become too much for them and they make their tragic exit. My experience of suicide taught me to be extremely compassionate towards those who kill themselves. An infinitely merciful God could not wish to punish all suicides, I believe. Many are not entirely in command of their intellectual resources. The sheer intensity of their sufferings can be overwhelming. They cannot endure another moment of their pain.

Fortunately, in my case, I had sufficient maturity, an awareness of the purpose of life and a solid conviction that there was another and a vastly more wonderful life awaiting us beyond the grave. I was somewhere in my fiftieth year at the time. The spiritual world was and is a reality for me, together with its ultimate prospect of a blissful hereafter. Eventually I was able to discern the options in my cruel dilemma. I believed in eternity. I believed in the existence of God. I accepted that He was all knowing and that He was the creator of all. I struggled to abide by His commandments. I just couldn't murder myself. To do so would have been profoundly wrong, and I would be punished for all eternity. Somehow I held on and resisted the temptation.

One morning, on waking, I had a vision of the devastation that would be visited on my family if I committed suicide. This realisation injected the resolve that I needed. I immediately set about pushing suicide aside. Fortunately I was able to do just that by the grace of God. In doing so, I later discovered that each of these suicidal compulsions was a passing phase. Each episode eventually passed off. They were transient phenomena.

Some of us – more of us than we'd like to admit, perhaps – create realms of fantasy about our lives. We deliberately act out a fantasy in our external everyday lives. We imagine that we are this or that icon. We observe someone, or a combination of persons, whom we greatly admire and proceed to pretend to the world that this is the person we are. We dress accordingly, act as we imagine they would do, drive a car like theirs and generally put on a front that is based on our observations of impressive people. We become actors, actresses or poseurs. We conduct ourselves in an imaginary part, consciously or unconsciously. There were times in my earlier life when I did just that. I am grateful that they were no more than phases, and I eventually recognised them for what they were and discarded them. The problem is that when such fantasies may usefully be torpedoed, we may not know where to turn. We lose our way in life and can become vulnerable. Such vulnerabilities can create the climate of suicide. Better to keep our feet solidly on the ground and be our real selves.

In retrospect, the suicidal state was a frightening ordeal. Interestingly while in the situation of planning to commit suicide, I experienced no fear. My mind was entirely focused on self-destruction. Coincidentally, as I originally typed these very words, I was preparing to attend the funeral of a friend. It had been death by suicide.

Later I heard that a note had been left for the family. The circumstances of my friend's life had been enormously difficult. There had been a succession of devastating setbacks. Because of my recovery from depression, I had been recommended to this person as someone who might be of help. We conversed by phone, and, in time, we became friends. We also exchanged correspondence. In my letters, I used every argument that I could muster against taking one's life. I failed to disturb my friend's mindset, though. I even had prayers offered for a change in her mind. I referred to my own experiences. But it was as if an invisible wall stood between us.

One day, I received a phone call telling me that this friend was dead. A week or two later, I received a letter in her handwriting, written shortly before committing suicide. 'There's no other way,' it said. I wasn't overly surprised. Our relationship had endured for four years or so. Perhaps between us we had exhausted its potential for a conversion. Life had flowed strongly for her for several years, during which too much of her was selflessly given away in helping another person, a fatally ill parent. Latterly, her life had been hell on earth. The evolving circumstances seemed to have been extraordinarily negative. This sufferer has surely gone to a better life, I believe, and I pray that an infinitely merciful God will not hand down eternal punishment to such an unfortunate person.

My depressive friend's sad and lonely death emphasised my own extraordinary good fortune. Surprisingly, I wasn't greatly upset by her going. I had recognised the inevitability of her end. 'Stunned' might be a better word. I had done what I could. I had written numerous supportive letters. I had prayed for her healing, and asked others to pray for her. God knows best.

I don't think that suicide is a symptom of depression – it isn't an easy way out of difficulties. Rather, I believe that it is a consequence of the extraordinary level of suffering endured by some depressives. I'm baffled by the degree of compulsion to end one's life that can occur, and I wouldn't remotely wish it on anyone. Neither would I condemn those who commit suicide. Of course, there are instances of people taking their lives when faced with a dramatic reverse in their material circumstances, and to some observers such an act can seem a waste. I would never condemn any suicide, though. How could I?

Depression and Work

Work inevitably entails stressful periods and events. Set-backs arise. Some people are so formed that they cope readily with these, taking them in their stride. Others seem to revel in the challenges of disruptions. Unfortunately, stress exacerbated my illness. Maybe I wasn't a stress-resistant type.

Not knowing precisely when my illness commenced, I can't be certain of the extent to which stress precipitated its onset. Certainly the break-up of the practice that my father had founded contributed, but the depression had already arrived by that time. As an employee, I coped reasonably with stress. Maybe the increasing responsibilities in life and work played their part in accelerating the arrival of the depression.

Following my cure, I did encounter severely stressful situations on a number of occasions. While they were extremely uncomfortable, there were no untoward ill effects. My cure stood firm.

Looking back over my career, it is obvious that the worst periods of my depression coincided with the most challenging phases in my profession. Prolonged levels of significant stress took their toll. They wound up the symptoms of my depression, and there was little I could do about this. Just as ambition can fuel demanding challenges, in my instance, my ambitious nature positioned me right in the path of oncoming stresses. I was lucky to have lived in the era of pharmaceutical research and manufacturing. My daily diet of their pills and capsules kept me going.

On reflection, I'm still surprised at my enduring capacity for work. I appreciate the extent to which work-related obligations helped to keep me going. Once, a friend from my cycling and university years questioned me about it. 'But you took on big public commissions and you were depressed. How did you do such things? I never knew that you were a depressive,' he exclaimed. He was well versed in depression, as his parents cared for a son of close friends who was severely affected by depression, and my friend had spent many hours chatting to him and knew that he had become unable to function usefully. So, he was familiar with the workings of the depressed mind.

While we were talking on the phone, I was conscious that he was terminally ill. We had been good friends during our university years. He had been a stellar racing cyclist. 'We used to be friends. You put me aside somehow. Why?' he interjected.

I had been dreading this question. 'My depression was part of it,' I lamely explained. I hadn't known of his past familiarity with depression, and he was astonished at my revelation. Our conversation took a turn for the better and we reminisced onwards covering a broad spread of our lives.

When I put the phone down, my secretary rushed into my room. 'What happened on that call?' she asked. 'You were hours on the phone. Has something serious happened somewhere?' I demurred as best I could.

Ultimately, on being cured, I seemed to have a choice. Would I return to work? Stressful situations would inevitably arise. They might well precipitate the return of depression, despite my acupuncturist's assurances. I pondered this apparently delicate choice. At the same time I was grappling with the unexpected confusion of living in a world free of all traces of depression. This proved to be a complex change. At times, it caused confusion. A familiar piece of my life was missing. The resultant void, most welcome though it was, disturbed me. It was as if I had lost an element of my very being.

In time, practicalities dictated that I return to work. I simply couldn't afford to retire. I was in my fifties and that is not the best time to make such a career change. In any event, the prospect of leaving my familiar work scene created its own doubts.

My underlying concern was the stability of my cure. Would it endure and stand up to the pressures and stresses that I had previously known? My acupuncturist reassured me with good-humoured conviction: 'Not alone will you cope, but you'll go on getting better and better. Anyway, in the unlikely event that the worst should happen to you, I'll be here.'

As it happened, I continued to work for a further eight years, up to my retirement at the age of sixty-five. Ironically the most grievous source of stress in that period arose following my departure from work. Leaving the firm I had founded was a deep wrench. There had been times when I didn't believe that I would survive to being pensioned. The prospect of death had for a long time loomed menacingly. There had also been those times when it even beckoned as a refuge.

Strangely I experienced little or no resentment at the illness that so dominated my working years. Neither did I have regrets about my career. Unquestionably my life was difficult. Inevitably and sadly, it was extremely difficult for my wife. Depression can grievously afflict a depressive's partner in life. To a lesser extent, it affected a few people who worked closely with me. Only those working in close contact with a sufferer can appreciate the frustration and exasperation of coping with a colleague borne down by depression.

Suggestions for Coping with Depression

What follows are suggestions based on my personal experiences. My knowledge of the illness reflects no more than my prolonged and painful encounter with it. I endured it for at least thirty years of my life, possibly longer. Despite the negative aspects of the experience, I remain intrigued by its effects and its complexity. I suppose the fact that I survived and was cured twice lends some measure of authority to my writing.

My cure endured for eighteen years. While I read everything I found on the illness, I didn't explore authoritative medical sources. There was a good reason for this apparent lapse. The necessary energy and willpower would not have been available to me. In working on this book, time and again I regretted that I hadn't kept a diary of the illness and its manifestations.

Accepting the Challenge

Step one for those readers who may be depressives has to be the resolve to find the strength and objectivity to accept the challenge that one is inescapably suffering from depression. This is not easy. It can be difficult to reach acceptance. For several years, I remained in denial, deluding myself time and again that I had been cured. A portion of my mental processes was malfunctioning, and I was thinking neither clearly nor objectively. It was simply that I didn't want to be ill. I wasn't really hearing all that my doctor was telling me. I didn't wish to.

Choosing Medical Advisers

For anyone suffering from depression, the choice of medical advisers is vital. Apart from qualifications, the interpersonal chemistry is most important. You must be comfortable with and have confidence in your medical consultants. Ask the right questions so that you can be satisfied that you are entrusting yourself to the best. Ask your GP why he or she is recommending a particular psychiatrist or specialist. If on the first encounter with the psychiatrist you are in any way uneasy, try someone else. A second and even a third opinion may be prudent.

Don't be overly compliant. For instance, be sure to query the whys and wherefores of a change of medication. However, once you are happy with your adviser, be fully compliant with all that he or she prescribes. Don't mess about with the taking of medications. They won't work for your benefit unless you stick to the instructions and complete each entire dosage. Some patients apparently never do this. This kind of casualness dismays me.

You must believe in your doctors. Recognise that well-meaning relatives and friends are not necessarily experts in the medical field. If they happen to mention something that appears to have merit, tell your doctor and your psychiatrist and listen carefully to their opinions. We all fall prey to half-listening, but it is crucial that you hear precisely what you are being told. Give all of your attention to your medical advisers during consultations.

Adopting the Right Attitude

Attitudes are so important. You must genuinely desire to be cured. Although it may sound strange, some depressives don't wish to be healed, as I had been told by my psychiatrist. 'Having one's back to the wall' is a familiar phrase, and a depressive's back is very much up against the wall. There remains only one way ahead in life. It is forward if you are to lead anything like a normal life. You must be utterly determined to keep going somehow, just as if the illness didn't exist. In a way, you must surrender to the actuality of depression. This does imply changing some of your habits.

Finding Useful Activities

Occupy your spare time in good and useful activities. Hobbies are invaluable. Anything that activates and absorbs the mind fully has to be beneficial. It helps to displace the worst symptoms of your illness, even if it's for only a brief period at a time. Read inspirational works. Classical music is an instance of good company just as appropriate as a good book can be. Also, get out and about and into the great outdoors as often as you can. Nature certainly helped me, and it is there for everyone's enjoyment. The sense of space and unchanging solitude and peacefulness can work wonders.

Be both active and involved. Voluntary work, as well as being beneficial to other people, also brings its own rewards: 'It is in giving that we receive.'

Make sure that there is an element of having-to-do in your life and even a sense of urgency at times. The latter fuels energy. You will gain inner strength in the very doing itself, as well as being distracted from the depression.

For example, as discussed in the first part of this book, I

found it vital to get out and about in the fresh air, to exercise regularly and maintain contact with nature. Once committed to this discipline, positive possibilities will be revealed. The mind will function better.

In a way, in the early years of the illness, I moped in the face of depression's menacing and overbearing presence. 'Wallowed' might be a better word. I felt sorry for myself. Several years elapsed before I recalled the phrase, 'God helps those who help themselves'. Once I did recall it, I picked myself up, pulled myself together and set about constructively combating the illness. In the first instance, I applied myself seriously to prayer. Later, I resorted to strenuous exercise and found the effects to be beneficial, as I have mentioned elsewhere.

I was physically well equipped through extended exercising over most of my earlier years. My preparations included schools rugby, fifteen years of competitive cycling, intermittent climbing, skiing annually and ten years of orienteering. While I suggest physical activities, it is important that your doctor's approval is obtained. However, walking is a more benign form of exercise and one that is available to all states and ages. Today, because of the realities of age, I walk, and I believe that it may in some way be related to reflexology. The feet are pressured at each footfall. These intermittent pressures react with the body's organs. This is a possible explanation of certain of the benefits of walking.

Self-discipline is vital. It can be acquired by practice. Regular exercising generates physical strength and energy, both crucial to improving one's willpower.

The Power of Prayer

Prayer was crucial as far as I was concerned. It is a matter of personal belief and conviction, and I was fortunate in believing in God. As well as desiring to be cured, it is important to pray continuously for a healing. If you pray, it is essential to believe that God does hear your prayers. Don't forget to thank Him in anticipation of His granting your request. Be bold enough to demand a cure.

I believe that He heard all my prayers. However, I also believe that He acts in His own manner and time. I accepted entirely that He was testing my belief when he took so long to respond to my prayers and those of my wife and my mother, in particular, and also of all those others whom I had asked to pray for me. I had read sufficient of the lives of saints and mystics to realise that God works in His own ways and in His very own time, often setting trials for those whom He loves most. I don't necessarily include myself among these. I'm a very ordinary sinner, but I do believe that God heard me. Looking back, I believe that there were several incidents of divine intervention — minor miracles if you like — along the way, and that these led me eventually to my recovery.

The Importance of Friends

Of course, sympathetic and empathetic friends matter, just as emotional props do. I was fortunate in this regard as my story recounts. One of these friends was a priest who first entered my life while I was at junior school. He was then the diocesan examiner, an awesome figure in the minds of children. In much later years, he kindly unravelled difficulties that arose when our eldest daughter was marrying a non-Catholic, and he attended her wedding.

A gifted conversationalist, he was equipped with an astonishing awareness of life. With him it was possible for me to reveal my innermost difficulties and apprehensions, and so gain useful directions and relief. Once, I met him on the Dublin–Cork train, and our conversation became so absorbing that I was absolutely astounded when I realised we were entering Cork station.

At a later stage again, he contacted me about an unusual problem concerning an existing church building. I was fortunate in being able to resolve it. We went on to become close friends and used to meet regularly for lunch when we had many heartfelt exchanges. During his final years, he corresponded with me from his bed in a nursing home. I treasured his letters, each of which generated intense anticipatory joy on their arrival. When I visited him, he often recounted remarkable and inspiring insights. I continue to wonder at the power that directed me to these encounters. I can only believe that they were instances of divine intervention.

Being Positive

Positive thinking creates its own inner reflected positivism in those who act positively. Yes, it's a stern battle when you are a depressive. Transcending the awful symptoms of depression is not easy, but it is possible, sometimes. Many successful people do just that, and there are recorded examples from many walks of life. These people appear to lead normal lives despite the hidden illness that weighs them down. Don't permit pessimism to crowd your thinking. Don't even contemplate despair or allow it to insinuate itself into your thoughts.

I used to get a distinct upbeat buzz whenever I was in the company of confident, positive and successful people. Those I met seemed to exude a tangible aura of confidence. In my instance, there was often a temporary transfer of positivism. Keep good and upbeat company whenever possible. It really helped me. Such company can feed positive inspirations.

Living in the Present

Come into the present — that is, into the present moment. When you are in the present, you have sufficient for all your needs. Think well about this. At any one moment, you have all that you need for life. Leave tomorrow for dealing with the morrow's demands. There will be a sufficiency for your needs when you arrive there. Reflect on this and its truth will eventually emerge. There are many excellent books on the topic of living in the present.

Being Yourself

I recommend that you be yourself. Being yourself in all circumstances can be challenging, and achieving this is part of the contest of life. It demands considerable strength of purpose, but it is possible. It avoids a great deal of trouble, not to mention inner confusion. It simplifies life. It implies being honest with both yourself and others. Each of us is gifted with a particular nature and personality at birth. Find out who it is that you truly are and live that part in life.

Persevering

Be patient. Persevere. Don't even consider giving up. Battle on and on and on with life, in the hope that improvement will come your way. If you don't, you're not giving life, or God, a chance. Get up and get out of bed as soon as you awake in the morning. It is absolutely vital. Things look better when you're standing up.

In my incomplete knowledge, there are few, if any, quick fixes as far as this illness is concerned. I eventually did find one such rapid fix in acupuncture, but it was presaged by twenty-odd years of effortful and dogged enduring and searching. It occurred to me recently that I never succumbed to despair. My hope for a cure endured. Perhaps it was a stubborn streak in my make-up. Whenever I faced an apparently impossible situation, I found the energy to face up to it.

If you decide to follow my example and opt for acupuncture, bear in mind that it does not work for everyone. I was one of the fortunate ones! Unfortunately, not everyone responds to the extraordinary effectiveness of this particular Chinese medicine.

Be Bold!

In conclusion, 'Be bold and great forces will come to your aid.' I came across this in a forgotten book. Whenever I steeled myself to do just this, these forces actually came to my aid. I wish you God's luck in your struggles. I empathise with you in your daily challenges.

Epilogue

As this book nears completion, my life progresses onwards towards the inevitability of death. No trace lingers of that incredible, majestic sense of release on being cured. I am well grounded in the real world of today, and there is little out of the ordinary in my days.

Life, for both my wife and me, has simplified. The pace of events has eased. We rise early, breakfast and attend Mass in the local parish church. I spend most mornings at my desk, and enjoy my less strenuous workout on three afternoons. Between times and among other activities, I read widely. I have time nowadays to read reflectively. We travel on our vacations. The world continues to remain a wondrous place, but my desire for exploration sadly diminishes. Nevertheless, I continue to read about places I haven't visited so far.

Recently, my wife's health had suffered for a year or more. However, a misdiagnosed hip problem was resolved successfully by a replacement, and she walks normally once again. I thank God for that. As I write, she is back to her energetic and organised self, occupied with family, golf, bridge, her circle of friends and family.

All our children are married, and life evolves onwards in the third generation of our family. Our sixteen grandchildren keep us in touch with emerging generations, and I find an odd depth of richness in observing them and noticing little things in them that had escaped me when our children were young. It's like witnessing the development of life for a second time. When observing the youngest ones, I marvel at their very nature, comprising truth, consciousness and bliss, and how this is expressed every now and again in all its glories.

The bigger challenges that can occasionally confront our sons and daughters invariably become our worries. Parents do not escape to a carefree never-never land, as I believed many long years ago. The fairy tales that I loved misled many with the words, 'and they lived happily ever after.' For myself, though, I'm well and content — for the most part. Time flies. My contemporaries also remark on this.

In completing this book, I have passed another significant milestone. Twenty-one years have elapsed since the depression lifted in 1987. Since my retirement from my profession some eight years later, this book has taken up a goodly portion of my time.

My health has remained good throughout, with that one stumble along the way. It was a useful warning shot across my bows. The ego can be overly ambitious at times. Consequently I have set definite limits as to what tasks I will entertain in future.

In my seventy-seventh year, I have eased up on my beloved outdoor activities. I no longer ski. My technique improved year by year, and in the penultimate year I skied as never before. However, the conditions were absolutely perfect on that occasion. The final year was not great — I seemed to have lost a subtle measure of balance. I fell too often. I liked to believe that this was related to the carving skis that I was using. They were fashionable, but I didn't like them. Maybe the years really were catching up on me. In reality, this presaged a balance/foot problem. It was eventually solved by neurosurgery.

My hill-walking has ceased. I was experiencing difficulty

in keeping pace with my walking group. Diminishing stamina imposed its humbling constraints. Minor injuries along the way didn't help. I told myself that I have to admit that the years are inevitably taking their toll. My exercising now comprises three walks weekly at least. I experienced minor foot problems for a period, but fortunately they are on the mend.

What of the future for depressives? Despite my ignorance of the complexities of the workings of the human body and mind, I would be optimistic in the longer term. The bodily energy that activates both mind and limbs suggests itself as a possible pathway along the route towards a cure for depression. Those explosive bursts of pain and energy I felt whenever my acupuncturist's needle struck the appropriate point on a meridian just had to be a good sign.

I remind myself that the great thing in my life is that I am no longer a ten per cent person, one of those ten per cent of the population who are depressives. It troubles me that I can take this gift for granted. There are times when I'm even dissatisfied with life. That is nothing but ingratitude.

Looking back, I have been extraordinarily fortunate. *Deo Gratias.*